CAUGHT'YA!
Grammar with a Giggle

Jane Bell Kiester

Caught'ya!
Grammar with a Giggle

Copyright© 1990, 2001, 2003 Jane Bell Kiester

All Rights Reserved

Second Edition.

Cover Design: David Dishman
Illustrations: Ralph Knudsen

The author appreciates comments and suggestions. Please contact her through the publisher.

Library of Congress CIP data

Kiester, Jane Bell, 1945-
    Caught'ya! Grammar with a Giggle/ by Jane Bell Kiester

Includes bibliographical references

ISBN 0-929895-04-5 $17.95

PE66.K5 1990
428'.007--dc20   90-30405

10   9

Also by Jane Bell Keister
    Caught'ya Again! More Grammar with a Giggle
    Elementary, My Dear! Caught'ya Grammar with a Giggle for Grades 1-3
    Giggles in the Middle: Caught'ya Grammar with a Giggle for Middle School
    The Chortling Bard: Caught'ya Grammar with a Giggle for High School
    Blowing Away the State Writing Assessment Test

Maupin House publishes innovative professional resources for K-12 language arts educators.

PO Box 90148
Gainesville, FL 32607
Phone: 800 524-0634 or 352-373-5588. Fax: 352-373-5546.
E-mail: info@maupinhouse.com. Visit us at www.maupinhouse.com.

This book is dedicated with a grin to Catherine Berg, Kren Kurts, and Mary Ann Coxe, three blunt-edged thorns who prodded me to write, and with love to Chuck who still loves me despite the writing.

TABLE OF CONTENTS

PREFACE

This is a "how-to" book. First and foremost, the message is "how-to" help students master the mechanics of language. What makes this book different and Mrs. Kiester's method effective is the second "how-to" — how to develop an enjoyable, encouraging, communicative relationship with students that is based on the learning activity. The soap opera suspense of the Caught'ya storyline, the good-natured teasing by both teacher and students, and the value of built-in success for every student create a situation where the relationship becomes a part of the effectiveness of the strategy.

This last "how-to" has a supplementary benefit. In effective classrooms, teachers immediately begin instruction when the bell rings. Mrs. Kiester shows how to accomplish this with her Caught'ya activity. While students complete the exercise, the teacher can check attendance or homework.

How well do these "how-to's" work? When I observe classrooms where teachers are using Caught'yas, I see students entering the classroom knowing the first order of business. Hallway chatter is quickly transformed to a curiosity about that day's Caught'ya. The friendly banter between teacher and students about the Caught'ya sets the tone for an amiable atmosphere where learning is important. The success of all students puts them on an equal footing to begin the next activity. The Caught'ya is a management technique with an affective bonus.

Finally and most importantly, to you wonderful teachers of English and for all of us who value the beauty as well as the function of the well-written word, a daily Caught'ya seems to inculcate the beauty as well as the mechanics of the English language. In our middle school we saw a remarkably significant increase in seventh grade standardized test scores in language mechanics after we initiated the Caught'ya at that level. No scientific study was conducted and, in fact, our comparison considered scores of two different groups of students. However, no similar increases were noted in other areas of the test, and we can point to no other variable which might have been responsible for such a specific gain.

If it is hard to imagine your students enjoying grammar, punctuation, vocabulary, and parts of speech, then introduce yourself to Jane Kiester's Caught'yas. Have some fun; create your own storyline or expand on the excellent examples she provides. Then introduce them to your students. Have fun doing that too, and your students will soon be excited about the story and will try assiduously to avoid your "Caught'ya." That's when the giggling starts.

Jacquelyn S. Cake, Ed.D.
Assistant Principal
Westwood Middle School
Gainesville, Florida

ACKNOWLEDGEMENTS

I especially wish to thank my mother, Perra S. Bell, and my husband, Charles L. Kiester, for their careful, painstaking editing of the manuscript. I also want to thank my fellow teachers: Catherine Berg, Kren Kurts, Carol Harrell, and Laurel Harb. They loved my Caught'yas, helped me polish them, and gave me encouragement.

Catherine Berg, whose teaching and judgement I deeply respect, was the one who urged me to widen my classroom and to present my idea to other teachers. Jacque Cake, vice-principal at Westwood Middle School, very kindly wrote the preface and has been an ardent supporter of the Caught'ya since I first introduced it to her in 1985. Her enthusiasm and administrative support have given me the courage to keep trying new ideas with my students. Mary Anne Coxe, the English Supervisor for Alachua County, gave me the opportunity to present my ideas to other teachers at local writing seminars.

Jacque Cake, Renée Hannen, Kren Kurts, and Judith Wade read the finished manuscript, made constructive comments, and laughed in all the right places. Lea Franz supplied vital moral support and made me exercise my body. Robert and Julie Graddy of Maupin House Publishing gave me the freedom to have this book published the way I wanted it to appear. I feel extremely fortunate to have found a publisher who firmly believes that every book is precious and that authors do know what they are doing.

Finally, I wish to acknowledge the help of all of my students over the past sixteen years. They have been my inspiration and my guinea pigs. They willingly provided me with examples for this book. They laughed at my jokes, tolerated my occasional gaffes, unabashedly enjoyed most of my experimental units, and have added a special meaning to my life.

INTRODUCTION

Frustration is Really the Mother of Invention

For eight and one-half years I was an elementary or a middle school English teacher with a big problem. How could I teach grammar, literature, spelling, mechanics, usage, vocabulary, drama, thinking skills, research skills, study skills, listening skills, handwriting, speech, proofreading, poetry, social skills, creativity, career education, alphabetizing, bibliographies, letter writing, and most importantly, the writing process in one brief period a day for only 180 days? Various academic and social programs at the school even took some of those days away from me. I was very frustrated.

The bottom line was that my students did not seem to be retaining the grammar, mechanics, and usage skills I was teaching them. I used different methods such as Mastery Learning, the standard book method, individualized programs, and so on, but none of them really worked. My students passed my tests with flying colors, which made me feel wonderful, but what they had learned did not seem to carry over into their writing.

They also did not like language arts. They considered it boring no matter what antics or methods I tried. I often felt like an incompetent clown, resplendent in large shoes, baggy costume, and painted smile never getting any laughs no matter what trick she attempted. I, too, began to believe that language arts was destined to be dull.

Because these traditional (and non-traditional) methods of teaching the basics of English took so much time, I didn't have enough days left in the year to try all the great literature and writing units I wanted to teach. This thorny dilemma plagued me for eight years. Then fate threw another curve into the works.

After teaching at North Marion Middle School in Marion County, Florida for over eight years, I changed counties and grade levels and became a fifth grade teacher in a self-contained classroom at J.J. Finley Elementary School in Gainesville, Florida. I suddenly had to teach reading, math, social studies, science, art, and computers as well as all those disciplines listed above for English. In addition, I had a problem I'm sure many of you elementary teachers face. I had four reading groups and four math groups. The county mandated that at least twenty minutes per day be spent with each reading group.

Three things resulted. First, the rest of the students in the class had to be given seat work for an hour or more a day while I worked with the other groups. Second, I had even less time during the day to teach basic writing skills. Third, due to the other two demands on time, the teaching of language arts was relegated to seat work (usually grammar exercises in the book) with little or no teacher input. I felt helpless and ineffective as an English teacher. This increased level of frustration finally drove me to find a solution.

I remembered from education classes at the University of Florida that Piaget had insisted that it was ineffective to teach formal grammar to students who were not at the stage of formal operation. I also knew that my fellow teachers had been drilling the same skills into my students' heads for the four years before they reached me, yet they still had not mastered these skills. Because of my experience in teaching middle school, I also knew that this would continue for at least another three years without much carryover into student writings.

Research since 1952 concludes that most high school students are not ready to retain any grammar or to apply its usage to their writing. This research also determines that teaching grammar, mechanics, and usage straight out of a textbook is not effective. (Elgin, 1982) Students do not learn much practical usage or application of language skills by doing exercises in books (except to pass a test at the end of each unit). In other words, students who learn a skill by completing textbook exercises and who test successfully in October seldom seem to retain that skill through November, let alone apply it to their writing.

Research also shows that a "learning by doing" approach is more effective than analyzing those textbook sentences which are never very much fun anyway. Learning by doing means sentence combining, expanding, and modeling good writing. Research also indicates that in order to be retained, skills need to be practiced continuously through writing and proofreading. I barely had enough time in the year to cover each skill once!

I also knew that language arts did not have a reputation for being a "fun" subject. Students thought that language arts classes were synonymous with boring. I was determined to change this image. Full of desperation, idealism, and enthusiasm, yet afraid to throw away that expensive textbook my county had so kindly provided me, I started searching for a solution in earnest.

I looked at various texts. They proved to be just that — textbooks with textbook exercises. I wrote a year-long program which I used to teach English. This program used textbook exercises coordinated with a newspaper activity and a writing assignment for each English skill. (Kiester, 1981) I tried this approach and found it more successful than any previous program, but I did not get the results I craved. We were still doing the textbook exercises, and the writing activities were stilted to force the use of the stressed skill.

Students were a bit happier with language arts, but their enthusiasm did not match mine. To make matters worse, the time for reading groups was being shortened. I knew my principal would not be thrilled with this.

Finally, in a flash of I-don't-know-what, the idea of the Caught'ya came to mind. I am a natural ham actress with a flair for the dramatic anyway. I love to laugh (I think that's why I'm addicted to middle school teaching). I write short stories and still dream of writing "the great American novel" someday, so this idea seemed perfect.

I tried my frustration-born idea on my unsuspecting fifth graders and experienced a very surprising result. They loved it! Still insecure, I continued the textbook exercises during reading group time to salve my conscience and to provide the busy work necessary to keep my students quiet. Toward the end of the year, however, I even abandoned this last attachment to tradition, giving my students "fun" writing assignments instead. My students and I were hooked! We all looked forward to our five to ten minutes a day of English grammar and usage practice.

After three more years of Caught'yas for my fifth graders, I returned to teaching middle school at Westwood Middle School in Gainesville, Florida. I continued to use the Caught'yas with even more success. A wonderfully inventive colleague of mine, Catherine Berg, helped me refine and polish the idea into the Caught'ya grammar that is explained in Chapter 2. Both of our classes loved it! Other teachers, encouraged by administrators and parents who liked what Catherine and I were teaching, began using the idea and adapting it to suit their own personalities. It worked in their classrooms as well.

All this happened over nine years ago. Since then, the idea of the Caught'yas has caught on among many more of my colleagues (at *all* grade levels) in Alachua County, Florida. Indeed, after my presentation at the Florida Council of Teachers of English conference in 1987, many more Florida English teachers in grades three to twelve successfully use the Caught'ya in their classrooms. The idea has been so successful, and the carryover into student writing so great, that in 1989 Alachua County incorporated the Caught'ya method of teaching English skills into the county's middle school curriculum guide.

While I am aware that the current trend is to abandon the teaching of grammar entirely, my many years of classroom experience have taught me that if you don't provide a model, students won't learn the concepts. I rarely ever "red pen" errors in my students' writing. That is the quickest way to destroy a budding love of writing. Instead I correct their Caught'yas. They quickly learn proofreading skills as well as grammar and usage, and they consistently and enthusiastically apply that learning to their writing.

I believe that it is like preventive medicine or a flu shot. Given the daily five minute injection by a method that only induces giggles and successes, students cease making egregious errors in their writing and consider English their favorite class.

My vice-principal insists that she also saw a dramatic improvement in the achievement test scores of our seventh grade students when the entire seventh grade began using Caught'yas. The evaluation method fosters success and totally eliminates failure among even the weakest students. As a result, language arts now has become a popular class where some students experience their first academic triumphs.

Finally, look at the chart at the end of this introduction. The Caught'ya takes care of grammar, mechanics, usage, vocabulary, letter-writing skills, cultural values, listening skills, handwriting, proofreading skills, editing skills, test-taking skills, and some spelling! The Caught'ya allows a teacher to cover almost half of the chart in only five to ten minutes a day of a class period. The bulk of each period then can be spent doing what is more enjoyable — reading literature and writing creatively. The Caught'ya allows English teachers to put the emphasis in their language arts programs back where it should be.

Needless to say, I have been tickled by the success and popularity of the Caught'ya among my fellow teachers, but we teachers find that our students are even more delighted. Once they used to groan their way through grammar; now they giggle their way into correct writing. What a nice change!

Language Arts Curriculum

As an exercise to illustrate a common teacher frustration, I have clustered all the things English teachers are expected to teach during the course of a year. I have left some blank spaces because I'm sure that you can think of more.

This sobering exercise points out the need to spend more school time on language arts or the need to develop a more efficient method to teach the basic English skills. Caught'yas combine at least a dozen of these skills into a five-minute-a-day exercise which also settles your class immediately. That's why the idea catches on quickly.

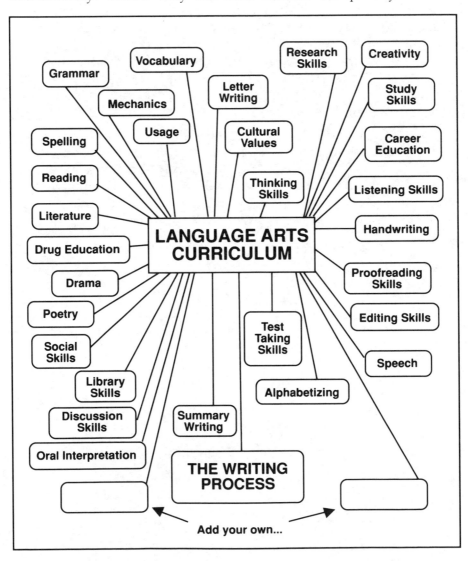

CHAPTER 1

What is a Caught'ya and How Does it Work?

The bell rang. Students poured out of my classroom into the quickly filling hallway. Other students, like streams of multi-colored water flowing into a muddy river, moved into the hall from open doorways nearby. Voices of varying pitches rumbled, squeaked, and yelled down the corridor.

"I'm goin' to get you after school!" yelled one small eighth grader to a foot-taller youngster beside him.

More voices blended in as the two students mixed with others in the now crowded hallway and rushed past me. I stood in the doorway of my classroom, occasionally waving to students, sometimes dodging quickly moving bodies. I shrugged my shoulders in a silent plea to another teacher standing in her doorway across the hall. The stream of students continued.

"Hi, Mrs. Kiester! What's Hairy doing today? Does Bertha find him?" queried Kim, a short, bright-eyed young lady, as she swept past me into my room.

"Look for yourself," I answered.

"Aw, you always say that," said Adam, a portly seventh grader in glasses. "I hope Hairy destroys some more things today!"

"You have no heart," complained Jennifer, as she squeezed through the doorway past Adam. "Poor Hairy has had a hard time. How would you feel if your girlfriend deserted you like that? I bet you don't even have a girl. You're even uglier than Hairy. At least he doesn't wear glasses." A small chase ensued as Adam ran after her.

I glanced inside my classroom. Several small boys threw a Nerf ball into the basketball hoop on my podium. A few girls had their notebooks out and were writing in them. Five seventh graders were standing near the board. "I already see three errors. She's not going to catch me today," said Matt arrogantly.

"Yes, she will. She always does!" retorted Arefah. "I'm the one who always gets one hundred."

"That's only when she checks it," Matt returned. "She caught you yesterday. I heard her!"

I looked back down the hallway. The bodies were thinning out as the students moved into classrooms.

"Hi, Mrs. Kiester," greeted Lashandra as she hurried to her seat and opened her notebook.

I glanced into the classroom again. The basketball game had stopped. Most of the seventh graders were in their seats, notebooks open, staring at the board. On the board was the following sentence which invited grammatical corrections:

tusday

bertha searched everywhere and could not find hairy yet she still heard _dolorous_ sobs echoing through the trashed messy apartment

"Come see if you caught me, Mrs. Kiester," signaled Matt. "I'm already halfway finished."

As the tardy bell rang, Lashandra called out, "What's dolorous mean?"

"That's a good question," I said, as I shut the heavy brown door on the noise of the bell. "Does anyone know what it means? 'Bertha heard dolorous sobs.' What kind of sobs did she hear?"

"That's got to be super sad sobs if they're Hairy's," called out Dean.

"What was that word last week that Dean knew?" asked Trevor in awe of his friend.

"Ajar. It was ajar. That was the one that my dad said in his joke. When is a door not a door? When it's ajar," answered Dean proudly.

"I still don't get it," whispered Stephanie to Lashandra.

"It means open, dummy," Lashandra whispered back.

"No, I mean Dean's joke," puzzled Stephanie, turning her head again to face me at the board.

"How many mistakes are there in the Caught'ya today?" asked Arefah.

"Well, let's see," I stalled as I counted. "I think there are seven including the two in Tuesday. See if I'm right. Let me read it to you. 'Bertha searched everywhere and could not find Hairy, yet she still heard dolorous sobs echoing through the trashed, messy apartment.'" I made a sad face as I read about the sobs and grimaced as I read the part about the messy apartment. "I bet some of your rooms look like Hairy's apartment all the time." I heard a few groans of acknowledgement.

"I know there's no paragraph today," blurted out Adam.

"Why?" I asked.

"Because Bertha is still looking for Hairy in his apartment," Adam replied. "She's still in the same place doing the same thing as she was yesterday."

"That's right," I said, giving Adam one of my most winning smiles. "How many of you guessed that as well?" All hands went up. I smiled inwardly. I knew some had fibbed because I saw a few erasers surreptitiously moving on their papers. That was all right. The point had been made. There were fewer erasers moving than there had been the day before!

"Come see if you caught me," called Dean.

"No, come to this side of the room first," cried Arefah. "You're not going to catch me today!"

"Want to bet?" I teased with a grin. "Watch out for that compound sentence. I caught a lot of people on that yesterday, including you." Arefah laughed and ducked her head as I wagged my finger at her. "I know I'm going to catch you today, too," I added.

"No, you're not," retorted Arefah with a big, knowing grin. "I've already found it!"

I started moving around the room. I looked over Jennifer's shoulder. "Caught'ya," I said triumphantly.

"Where, where?" she asked.

"Look again in the second line. Is 'could not find Hairy' a complete sentence? Put your finger over the 'and' and check again to see if there is a complete sentence on both sides," I hinted.

I moved on to Dean. "I didn't catch you," I marveled. "Just you wait until tomorrow."

Dean made a face at me. "Put in another compound sentence. I dare you. I've got the idea now. You won't catch me again!"

I patted his back affectionately. "Maybe you're right."

I moved on to look at the next child's paper. I tapped Shannon's shoulder and smiled. "Caught'ya," I teased.

"Where?" Shannon asked.

"Look again," I replied. "I'm sure you can find it yourself if you're careful."

I moved on again to another student. "I caught Matt too," I sang. Matt bent his head over his paper, searching frantically.

"I found it!" Shannon yelled behind me. "Can I just correct it since I found it all by myself?"

I looked at her, smiled, and nodded.

I continued my walk through the class. I found a few more errors. Every time I found one, I gently tapped the child on the shoulder and said, "Caught'ya." Sometimes I stopped to give a hint. Sometimes I became frustratingly annoying and challenged the student to find the error himself. There were a few children whom I didn't "catch." I announced each loudly so the whole class could hear.

I reached Arefah. She had been gesturing wildly with a smug expression on her face. I looked at her paper.

"Well?" she asked.

"She'll catch you," Adam assured her.

"Oh, pooey, I didn't catch you today!" I announced to Arefah loudly enough so Adam could hear.

"I knew it," Arefah snorted in Adam's direction. "She'll catch you on the two adjectives."

Adam poured over his paper before I could get there. I saw him make a mark on it. He sighed a sigh of relief and looked anxiously at me. When I glanced at his paper, I quietly pointed to the word "Tuesday." Adam quickly capitalized the word, wincing at the same time. I patted him on the back, smiled widely, and announced. "I didn't catch Adam today either."

Adam's round brown face split into a wide grin. "That's the first time in over a week," he sighed. "I'll do it again, Mrs. Kiester. Just you wait!"

I ruffled his hair. "I'm sure you're right, Adam. You're doing better and better." He smiled back at me. My teacher's heart melted, and I knew once more why I liked my profession.

I glanced at my watch. Five minutes had elapsed since the bell had rung. I quickly checked the rest of the class. "Caught'ya. Caught'ya. Oh, I didn't catch Lashandra today!"

Lashandra beamed at the news.

I ended with Stephanie. I noticed that she was finally capitalizing the first word in the sentence. I smiled at her. "I caught you, Stephanie," I said very quietly so no one else could hear. "But I'm so proud of you! Look, you remembered to capitalize the first letter of the sentence and put a period at the end. Good for you! Pretty soon, you'll get the rest too," I encouraged.

I skipped to the front of the classroom and up to the board. "What am I going to do?" I wailed. "You all are getting better and better. I'll just have to make the sentences harder and harder." A collective groan rose from the class as I grinned evilly.

"O.K., let's check the Caught'ya, I said. "Where's the first error?"

About fifteen hands went up. I called on Adam. "You have to capitalize 'Tuesday.'" he said confidently.

The hands waved at me again. Adam continued. "You also need an 'e' in it to spell it correctly."

"Right," I said. I grabbed my yellow chalk (the sentence was in white chalk on the board), put three lines under the 't' in Tuesday, circled the word, and wrote in an 'e' above the circle. "Where is the next error?"

I called on Stephanie who was frantically waving her arm back and forth.

"'Bertha' has to start with a capital letter," she announced triumphantly, giving me a secret smile. I winked back.

I put three lines under the 'b.' "What else?" I queried. "Is there a comma after 'everywhere?'"

"No," called out about ten students at once.

"Why?" I persisted. "Tell us, Jennifer."

"Well," Jennifer hesitated. Then she said in a stronger tone, "Because it isn't a com... com..."

"Compound sentence," Dean finished for her.

"Right," Jennifer returned. 'Could not find Hairy' is not a sentence."

"Correct, Jennifer," I said as I drew a comma in the spot on the board, circled it, and marked through it with a delete sign. "What's next?" I continued.

Arefah put her hand up. "The comma in the compound sentence," she said. "Put a comma after 'Hairy' and before 'yet.'"

I put a comma in the appropriate place and circled it. "I can't fool you," I teased back. "Class, what part of speech is the word 'yet?'"

"Conjunction," yelled about twenty-five eager voices.

"What are the seven coordinating conjunctions?" I sang.

"And, or, nor, for, so, but, yet," the class chorused.

"Again," I sang.

"And, or, nor, for, so, but, yet."

"What can't you begin with one of these?"

"A sentence!" the class yelled back.

"I know where the next mistake is," blurted out Adam, unable to contain himself.

"Where?" I encouraged him to continue.

"Between the words 'trashed' and 'messy,'" he said.

"Why? What part of speech are those two words?"

"Because there are two adjectives with no 'and' between them," he said proudly.

"Right! Would there be a comma if the second adjective had been a color?" I probed.

Only a few hands went up. I called on Dean. "No," he said. "Not if the second adjective is a color or young or old." He beamed at the class.

"You forgot that there isn't a comma if the second adjective is part of the thing like a jet plane," Arefah threw in with a smug grin at Dean.

I put the comma between 'trashed' and 'messy,' circled it, and continued. "You're both right," I said. "Where's the last error?"

The class groaned as a whole, "A period at the end of the sentence."

"You never catch us on that anymore," crowed Adam.

"You're right," I smiled. "What's 'dolorous mean', class?"

"Sad," my students answered back.

I put the period in place on the board and circled it. "Now, class, mark your errors in a contrasting color, count the number of errors that you did not find on your own when you corrected the sentence yourself, mark that number in the right margin, and draw a line under today's Caught'ya, so we can put tomorrow's Caught'ya underneath it. Be very careful so you can get an 'A' on your Caught'yas for the week and get your name in the Caught'ya lottery. I looked at my watch. Nine minutes had elapsed since the tardy bell had rung. I was on schedule.

The students bent over their papers in earnest. "Now, put the Caught'ya paper in your notebook and get out a piece of paper. We're going to write again today......."

As I continued to explain the day's assignment, I smiled to myself and looked out at the faces of my students. They were smiling too, and listening, *really* listening to me!

The above story is a conglomeration of what happens daily in my regular seventh grade English classes. The same thing occurs in my advanced eighth grade class, only the discussions are a bit more sophisticated, the banter is a bit more barbed, and the sentence is a bit harder. What is this Caught'ya to which I keep referring?

The Caught'ya is an integrated approach to language skills that is fun, efficient, and effective. The basic Caught'ya is very simple, and it takes less than ten minutes a day to do. Essentially it is a sentence or two of an ongoing, funny story put on the blackboard or overhead three to five days each week. This sentence is laced with errors, errors that the teacher wishes to eliminate in her students' writing. Students write the Caught'ya as correctly as they can. Meanwhile, the teacher walks around the room and gives immediate feedback to individual students, providing mini-lessons if necessary. After most of the students have completed the sentence, the teacher returns to the board or overhead. The class checks the Caught'ya together, using proofreading symbols to mark errors missed. Students count the errors they missed the first time and mark the number in the margin. A skill has been introduced, reinforced or practiced, and maybe the class has enjoyed a giggle over the story or over the antics of the teacher.

The evaluation of the sentences is based on whether students catch the errors and mark them on their papers when the class goes over the Caught'ya, not on the errors caught the first time when students attempt to correct the sentence on their own. This way *every* student, no matter how weak he or she has been in English skills, can have success with the Caught'yas. Even a Stephanie can get an A+ on her paper.

A teacher can put a Caught'ya on the board every day or do only three or four a week. It does not matter, as long as the story line is not lost or forgotten. Skills can be repeated *ad nauseum* until every student in the class masters them or begs for mercy.

Students soon get used to entering the classroom and immediately settling down to write the Caught'ya. The Caught'ya routine shortens the "waste time" at the beginning of every period. Because students crave the individual feedback their teacher gives while they are working on the Caught'ya, they usually get to work very quickly.

Sometimes students help each other with the errors in the Caught'ya. I often hear whispered debates as to whether a comma should be put in a certain spot. This peer cooperation also makes the Caught'yas more fun and more effective. I often challenge individuals or an entire class, insisting that I will "catch them" that day.

Students weak in English skills especially love the Caught'ya because it eliminates any feeling of failure and frustration associated with language arts. Since Caught'yas are short, they can be completed even by those students with short attention spans. If I have an easy Caught'ya on the board, I deliberately check my weaker students so I can praise them for making no errors that day. I make a game out of it so that my students feel good about their work and are challenged to try their best. My reward is hearing two students arguing over a capital letter or whether a paragraph is needed, instead of discussing the latest fight in the hall. Students really seem to get into the Caught'ya sentences and strive to get them correct so that I don't "catch them."

It does not matter what grade you teach. This system works at any level. In my county there are teachers from grades three through eleven who use this method. It is up to you to change and modify the concept to fit your needs.

Do not worry if you are a shy person or feel that you are not naturally a ham actor. These Caught'yas will be successful in your classroom if you are at all enthusiastic about them. If it is not your style to cavort around the classroom, a simple touch or quiet word will suffice. Modify the Caught'ya concept to fit *your* personality.

Remember, many teachers have used the Caught'ya system with great success. All these teachers have different personalities. No two teachers present the Caught'yas in exactly the same way. The basic system works. Do what you feel comfortable doing with your students.

In subsequent chapters I explain how Caught'yas can be changed in innumerable ways, limited only by a teacher's imagination. When combined with frequent writing practice, responding, and editing, Caught'yas can replace traditional methods of grammar teaching with startling results. I knew Caught'yas worked when the reading teacher asked me why my students (and not others) consistently knew how to correctly punctuate quotes in their book reports. I had previously seen the same improvement in students' writing in my own classroom, but I had questioned those results because *I* had been looking for the transfer of skills.

In Chapter 2, I explain the ten basic steps necessary to set up a successful Caught'ya system in your classroom. Stop right here! As a teacher, I know what you're thinking. "Yoiks! Ten steps! Who in her right mind could (or would) go through ten steps in less than ten minutes?" Please don't get put off by the fact that there are ten steps. I have broken down the directions into *very* small components. One of the steps, for example, instructs you to write a sentence on the board. Three steps guide you to write your own story.

At the end of Chapter 2 is a one-page lesson plan so that you can keep it near you in your classroom for easy reference until you are comfortable with the Caught'ya grammar system. The detail in each step ensures that you fully understand the system. Since this is a book and not a workshop, I am not right there to answer your questions, so I have tried to anticipate anything you might ask.

As you read the next chapter, however, it is very important to remember three things. Keep everything positive, make those Caught'yas funny, and dredge up all the ham actor in yourself that you can muster for the five to ten minutes you do the daily Caught'ya.

 **CHAPTER 2**

The Caught'ya in 10 Easy Steps

Ten Easy Steps to a Successful Caught'ya

---

1. **Outline or choose story plot.**

2. Decide on skills and vocabulary word.

3. Compose daily sentence.

4. Write sentence incorrectly on board or overhead.

5. Students write Caught'ya as correctly as they can.

6. Walk around, commenting on students' Caught'yas.

7. Go to board and check Caught'ya with class.

8. Students mark mistakes with proofreading symbols.

9. Students count and indicate number of errors.

10. Collect Caught'yas at end of week.

STEP 1

 Beginners probably should use one of the basic story lines of the three sets of one hundred Caught'ya stories provided in Chapters 6, 7, and 8. Those of you who feel comfortable doing so can create the plot of an original soap opera or a silly story of your own.

Chapter 5 provides you with several story suggestions for elementary, middle, and high school classes. These are tried and true story lines made up by me, by a colleague, or by a group of teachers. It is best, of course, if you eventually come up with your own story, something that *you* know will appeal to your students.

Creative thought, however, is often elusive, especially at the beginning of the school year. It is also sometimes difficult to try an entirely new system. I know that the first time I use a new text or unit at school or a new recipe at home, I stick very close to the original until I feel comfortable. The first year that you use the Caught'ya system you might find it more comfortable to use either one of the plots listed in Chapter 5 or one of the three sets of one hundred sample Caught'ya sentences provided in Chapters 6, 7, and 8. After the first year of using this system, you probably will want to develop your own story.

When you do write your own plot, the story line should be in the form of a rough outline. At this point, *do not* write the story. You want only the bare bones of a plot. You will fill in the text during the year as you determine which skills your students need. One story per year is all that is needed, but the plot must be convoluted enough to support 100 to 180 sentences depending on whether you use the Caught'yas three, four, or five times a week.

One way of developing your own plot line is to draw upon stories you told your own children at bedtime, retell a story you remember from your own childhood, or revise a literary work to the level and interests of your students. The basic, gut-level soap opera works very well with the middle and high school set. Throw in a few love triangles, a couple of fights, and a wild party or two, and your students will beg to find out what is going to happen next.

Here is an example of the original outline of the plot for the Hairy Beast story. In Chapter 7 you can see how I used this outline to create one hundred Caught'ya sentences. Notice that the story is simple but leaves lots of room for expansion.

Hairy Beast and Friends (General Animal Hospital)

I.   Description and introduction of characters
    A.   Hairy Beast
        1.   Ugly, green fur, warts, animal of indeterminate origin and species
        2.   Sensitive, gentle personality, emotional
        3.   Lives with all others in Hogtown, Florida
    B.   Hilda Hippo
        1.   Corpulent, cruel, beautiful in Hairy's eyes, a two-timer
        2.   Not a nice hippopotamus that you'd want to bring home to mother

3. Always looks for what she doesn't have

4. Uses people (animals)

C. Wilfred Warthog

   1. A kind, non-aggressive warthog, makes mistakes

   2. Cares deeply about his friend Hairy

   3. Goes with Bertha Boa

D. Bertha Boa

   1. Your normal four-foot long boa constrictor

   2. Very kind-hearted, always wants everyone to be happy, extremely loving, very loyal to Hairy

   3. Goes with Wilfred Warthog

E. Eggbert Elephant

   1. A typical pachyderm with an extra long trunk

   2. Snooty, pompous, too good for Hairy and friends

   3. Likes parties, good times, and females

F. Various other characters will be invented as needed

II. Hairy is jilted by Hilda

A. Receives "Dear John" letter insulting his appearance

B. Rants, raves, cries, destroys things

C. Hides in his apartment

III. Bertha and Wilfred exchange letters and check out Hairy

A. Bertha slithers to Hairy's apartment to check

B. Hairy nowhere to be seen and Bertha looks everywhere

C. Letter - Bertha to Wilfred asking for help for their friend

D. Letter - Wilfred to Bertha saying he'll help

IV. Consolation of friend

A. Bertha sends flowers

B. Wilfred sends a note that is inadvertently insulting

C. Hairy, now doubly upset, rants some more

V. Wilfred goes to Hairy

A. Apologizes

B. Takes Hairy to Hilda to insult her

C. Goes back to Bertha for a talk (lots of conversation here)

VI. Hairy goes into deep hibernation to get over Hilda
  A. Goes to store
  B. Plans where to hole up
  C. Executes plan

VII. Wilfred and Bertha plan a party
  A. Food, etc. (conversation here)
  B. Invitations (introduce Eggbert as new in town and describe)
  C. Coerce Hairy into coming

VIII. Party
  A. Describe wild, wild party
  B. Hairy, Hilda, Eggbert among guests
  C. Hilda falls for Eggbert
  D. Hairy gets over Hilda
  E. Messy cleanup

IX. Ending
  A. Hilda and Eggbert go together briefly
  B. Hilda gets jilted and heads off to Tibet to try to change
  C. Hairy finds new girlfriend (possibly Bertha)
  D. Everyone but Hilda is happy

Another way to come up with a good, amusing plot is to brainstorm with your fellow teachers. Again, at this point you only want the basic plot outline, not the actual sentences. The more outlandish the plot, the better. You can't go very far in a story with only 150 sentences or so, hence simple soaps work best. Enjoy yourself! When Cathy Berg and I got together to create our story outline for the year, we laughed so much at our own silly ideas that we had as much fun as our students.

If you teach in a church school, you might want to use Bible stories for the plot. When I recently gave my workshop to a group of Adventist teachers, several of them suggested that using Bible stories might be perfect for their classes. I left them brainstorming which stories would be best to use for the Caught'yas at each grade level.

Parents who use the Caught'yas for home school use can base the story on personal experiences of their children. Familiar people and situations can be used. Children love to read about themselves. That is why my story for elementary school has blanks for students' names.

Whatever story you use, make sure that you can keep your students hanging so they can't wait for the next installment. Extra, juicy details can be provided in spelling practice sentences or in tests. (See Chapter 4 for details.) Poke fun at adults and keep the story amusing. You want your students to giggle! You also want to make them *want* to come to your classroom each day to find out what is going to happen next in the story.

Experience has taught me that students feel the story belongs to them. They are miffed if you use "their" story line with the following year's class. For this reason, I usually have two plots that I alternate from year to year. These plots create a bond between teacher and students, well worth the extra work. It becomes an "in" joke between you and your students since both of you are involved in plot development and character descriptions.

It is always a good idea, especially with advanced classes, to have the students help plan out the story line and name the characters. I always have a drawing contest to come up with pictures of the characters for our bulletin board. Not only does this solve the problem of filling one of your bulletin boards, but it also can involve some of your students whose work is seldom displayed. It helps those students feel as though you take them seriously since you are basing your description of the characters on their drawings.

You can base various writing assignments on your Caught'ya plot. What will happen next? Describe the wild party. Write a character sketch of one of the protagonists. Write a letter to one of the characters. Some of these ideas are explained in Chapter 4.

Ten Easy Steps to a Successful Caught'ya

1. Outline or choose story plot.

2. **Decide on skills and vocabulary word.**

3. Compose daily sentence.

4. Write sentence incorrectly on board or overhead.

5. Students write Caught'ya as correctly as they can.

6. Walk around, commenting on students' Caught'yas.

7. Go to board and check Caught'ya with class.

8. Students mark mistakes with proofreading symbols.

9. Students count and indicate number of errors.

10. Collect Caught'yas at end of week.

STEP 2

 Decide which skill(s) you wish to introduce, practice, review, or reinforce. You also need to choose a vocabulary word that you would like your students to learn.

Now that you have chosen or developed a basic story or outline, it is time to fill it in week-by-week. Decide what you wish to teach. It can be any skill. You may want to work on punctuating quotes, one of the comma rules, verb tenses, one of the irregular verbs, paragraphing, sentence combining, spelling, etc. I repeat and repeat *ad nauseum* skills that my students have not mastered until most of the class gets them. Students even plead with me to stop putting in a skill, "No more compound sentences!" or "Not another series!" or "Please, we know 'I' comes before 'E' except after 'C', and neighbor and weigh are weird. Enough!"

The lower the grade, the fewer the skills you want to include in each sentence. Take your cue from your students. Each class is different. This is the reason I do not give you a specific number of skills to include in each Caught'ya for each grade level. Judge your students yourself. If you have too many difficult skills in one Caught'ya sentence, your students will experience less success. If you don't stimulate them enough, your students soon will be bored.

Remember that student success helps make the Caught'yas fun. You also may want to make sure that you have a few days when there are no difficult skills in the sentence so that your slower students can get the sentence correct the first time and be encouraged. Even in my advanced classes, unless I am doing a review of previously mastered skills, I am careful not to overwhelm them.

Since one of the advantages of using the Caught'ya to teach English skills is that you easily can repeat and repeat the skills that *your* class finds difficult, it is best to write your own Caught'ya sentences rather than use those written by someone else. This is the one drawback to using my Caught'yas in Chapters 6, 7, and 8 or to using *Daily Oral Language*. (Neil and Papenfuss, 1982) If you use someone else's sentences, then you can't always address the particular needs of *your* students since the skills are already predetermined.

Despite this drawback, however, the Caught'ya sentences that I provide in Chapters 6, 7, and 8 are a good place to start the first year you use this method of teaching grammar. These Caught'yas have been classroom tested and will give you a feel for what works.

If you do decide to use one of my sets of one hundred Caught'ya sentences in Chapters 6, 7, and 8, you *can* change the sentences to suit your needs. Only one hundred Caught'yas are given, leaving room in the plot to add Caught'ya sentences of your own where and when you need them. For example, let's say your students need more practice with punctuation of quotations. If there is already a conversation among the characters, just write some more conversation. If you are working on letter writing format, you can write a short note into the plot. If you need more irregular verb practice, substitute some verbs in the plot. If your students still don't know how to capitalize a title correctly, have the characters read a few books, etc..

I usually use the mistakes my students make in their writing to indicate which skills I need to include in the Caught'yas. Some years, especially with advanced classes, I let the students come up with the plot. I decide on the skills and write the sentences. Every time I read my students' writing efforts, I keep notes on the mistakes I find, so I can include them in future Caught'yas.

You are entirely unlimited in deciding what you want to teach in the daily Caught'ya. If you wish to teach the parts of speech, tell your students to label them. Just keep the sentence simple. If you want to teach diagramming of sentences, write a sentence your students can diagram. Unlike the sentences in *Daily Oral Language*, the Caught'yas are sentences in an ongoing story. This way, you teach paragraphing all year long. Frequently you also can include the little errors that students constantly make, like spelling "a lot" as one word. After twenty or so repetitions, they begin to get it right.

You also need to decide on a vocabulary word to put in each Caught'ya sentence. I have found (after writing thousands of the sentences) that the easiest way is to decide on the vocabulary word after the sentence is written. At that point, I look at the sentence to see which word can be replaced by a more difficult synonym. If I don't find such a word, then I have to go back and revise the sentence, but usually a word comes to mind. I also find that I frequently consult a thesaurus. If you have a prescribed list of vocabulary words that you wish to include in the sentences, then I suggest that you keep that list in front of you as you write the Caught'yas and fit in the words wherever you can.

Please note that you can review vocabulary simply by repeating the words in subsequent Caught'yas. I also advise you never to make your students accountable for the vocabulary words. Instead, challenge them to use them in their writing. Instruct them to box the word if they wish to earn extra credit for its correct use.

As you read Chapters 6, 7, and 8, you will notice that some of the same vocabulary words are repeated in elementary, middle, *and* high school level sentences. Vocabulary words in the Caught'yas are intended for fun and enrichment. They are not bound to one grade. You only want to make certain that your students do not already know the words you use.

It is delightful to experiment with ten-dollar words. A fourth grader can fall in love with the word "lugubrious" as it rolls around on his tongue. Middle and high school students can enjoy adding that same sonorous word to their oral vocabularies and then using it in their writing. Since students are never tested on these vocabulary words, and they only get extra credit when they use them, they tend to experiment with them. The more difficult and interesting the word, the more the children like to use it. One seventh grade class of mine decided that they would never learn to spell "a lot" as two words, so they all adopted "a plethora" instead!

If you look at the student letters in Chapter 4 of this book, you will see that one of my weaker seventh graders used the word "dulcet." Needless to say, he got the extra credit! Just make sure that you introduce at least one vocabulary word in each Caught'ya sentence.

Ten Easy Steps to a Successful Caught'ya

1. Outline or choose story plot.

2. Decide on skills and vocabulary word.

3. **Compose daily sentence.**

4. Write sentence incorrectly on board or overhead.

5. Students write Caught'ya as correctly as they can.

6. Walk around, commenting on students' Caught'yas.

7. Go to board and check Caught'ya with class.

8. Students mark mistakes with proofreading symbols.

9. Students count and indicate number of errors.

10. Collect Caught'yas at end of week.

STEP 3

 Write the sentence or two that make up the Caught'ya. Be sure to include the skills you decided on in STEP 2. Don't forget the vocabulary word.

Now that you have the basic plot outline, have decided on the skills you want to include, and have a vocabulary word in mind, you are ready to write the text of the daily Caught'yas. Simply write a sentence (or two for higher grades) of the plot you created. Make sure that the sentence includes the skills you want and a vocabulary word. My seventh and eighth grade students, however, advise you to keep two things in mind. One, keep the Caught'ya short. Two, make the sentence funny.

I usually write a week or two of Caught'yas at once, so the continuity of the story is not broken. Do not write your daily Caught'ya sentence too far ahead since you may need to include another skill or repeat an already taught skill until mastery occurs. You might have to rewrite your sentences.

I try to keep the sentences simple. As suggested in STEP 2, after you have written a sentence, look at the words to see where you can substitute a more difficult vocabulary word. Again, make sure that you introduce at least one new vocabulary word in each Caught'ya.

After using the Caught'ya system for a while, you will become familiar with the skills that you want to include. You may find that you can use sentences from a previous year with only a few changes.

Writing the daily sentences is the hardest part of the Caught'ya system. This is why I have provided three sets of one hundred Caught'yas for you in Chapters 6, 7, and 8. If you decide to write your own, however, I suggest that you combine forces with your colleagues.

My fellow teachers and I have found that it often helps to divide the work load. We all analyze our students' writings for the skills we want, come up with a mutual list, decide on other skills that we also wish to include, and then take turns writing the sentences to fit the plot we chose. This community effort usually works best if one teacher writes the daily sentence, a week's worth at a time, for a month or six week period. In this way the continuity of the story can be kept more easily.

I also have worked with one other teacher to write the daily sentences. We found that we sometimes got a bit silly, but we certainly had fun. The sentences for the story in Chapter 7 were written this way. In this case, we usually wrote about three weeks worth at a time. Cathy Berg and I still refer to that year with grins on our faces. We got into the plot so much that we both dressed up as the main character for Halloween. I think our students caught our enthusiasm as well. This story continues to be popular among middle schoolers.

Intersperse difficult sentences with easy ones. You want to make sure that even your slowest student can have a few days when he gets the Caught'ya correct all on his own the first time. Just make sure that in STEP 6 you go to that student first if you have an easy sentence. The fact that you didn't "catch him" just once will encourage the slower student to try even harder in the future.

With experience, you will find that writing the daily sentence gets easier and easier. You even may want to revise a sentence as you put it on the board in the morning to include something that came up the previous day.

Again, keep those sentences short, amusing, and action packed.

Ten Easy Steps to a Successful Caught'ya

1. Outline or choose story plot.

2. Decide on skills and vocabulary word.

3. Compose daily sentence.

4. **Write sentence incorrectly on board or overhead.**

5. Students write Caught'ya as correctly as they can.

6. Walk around, commenting on students' Caught'yas.

7. Go to board and check Caught'ya with class.

8. Students mark mistakes with proofreading symbols.

9. Students count and indicate number of errors.

10. Collect Caught'yas at end of week.

STEP 4

 Write the sentence on the blackboard or on an overhead transparency.

Plot, skill, and actual sentence in hand, you are ready to present the Caught'ya to your class. You can write the Caught'ya sentence on the blackboard under an appropriate sign. I use a Halloween picture of a monster with the word Caught'ya written across it. I like to put my daily sentences on the blackboard so that I can revise them on the spot if I wish. I usually write the four sentences for the week on the board every Friday afternoon. This way I am not panicked early in the morning if someone calls an emergency meeting, or a parent comes by unexpectedly for a conference. I prefer the blackboard for the flexibility it gives me.

A friend of mine, Kren Kurts, swears by her overhead. After she writes the sentences, she puts them on overhead transparencies. She says that this makes less work for her in the long run, especially if she wants to reuse sentences another year. She writes the sentences in permanent marker and then corrects them in erasable marker.

Since I teach seventh *and* eighth grade English, I need two Caught'yas every day. This year I plan to write one on the board and try the other on the overhead. Try both methods to see what works for you. I hate to be at the mercy of audiovisual equipment on a daily basis, so I am uneasy about using the overhead this year, but I simply don't have the board space for two different Caught'ya stories at the same time.

When you write the sentence, wherever you choose to write it, be sure to box the vocabulary word very clearly. Write the sentence with all the errors you decided to include in STEP 2. You can put in some punctuation or leave everything wrong.

With younger students you do not want to include too many errors, or they will have no chance for success. They discourage easily. For example, you can write a sentence like this:

the teacher said, "i want you all to be very good today"

This provides the quotation marks and the comma that a fourth grader or a slower middle school student might miss, but it also provides a good discussion on where end punctuation belongs in a quote as well as what needs to be capitalized. It puts success well within the grasp of all your students. It also tailors the Caught'yas to your curriculum.

The more advanced the age group, obviously the more errors you can include. In my regular seventh grade classes I leave in most of the errors, but I concentrate on keeping the sentences simple. As the year progresses, I make the sentences more complicated with more errors.

Look at Chapters 6, 7, and 8 to see the sentences that I suggest putting on the blackboard. In these chapters I list the board sentences as well as the corrected versions of them for use in STEP 7. If you use these, and you feel your students need more help, then write part of the Caught'ya correctly.

Here's another suggestion that my students made. I took their advice, and I suggest you do as well. Regular students like having the number of errors in the Caught'ya listed beside it. They say that this makes them feel more secure. I have noticed that it really doesn't make much difference in the number of errors corrected, but if my students feel more secure with it, then it is worth counting the errors and putting that number on the board.

I have encountered one major problem with this suggestion. Correctly counting the errors in a Caught'ya is difficult! I make mistakes all over the place. It all works out in the end, however. My students are more than happy to correct me, and it tends to keep them more on task as they look for mistakes in my counting of the errors. I do not provide this service for my advanced classes. I have found that these super achievers sometimes get upset if they can't find the number of errors that I indicated.

If you are trying to teach parts of speech, simply put under the sentence, "Label the parts of speech." If you want to teach one part of speech, simply write under the sentence, "Circle all adverbs." You can change the daily instructions with a little note. This is one of the features that makes the Caught'ya system so flexible.

There is one more very important thing you must do. When you write each day's Caught'ya sentence on the board or overhead, write the day of the week you plan to do that sentence. Write the day incorrectly or don't capitalize it. This serves several functions which will be further explained in STEP 5.

Ten Easy Steps to a Successful Caught'ya

1. Outline or choose story plot.

2. Decide on skills and vocabulary word.

3. Compose daily sentence.

4. Write sentence incorrectly on board or overhead.

5. **Students write Caught'ya as correctly as they can.**

6. Walk around, commenting on students' Caught'yas.

7. Go to board and check Caught'ya with class.

8. Students mark mistakes with proofreading symbols.

9. Students count and indicate number of errors.

10. Collect Caught'yas at end of week.

STEP 5

 Immediately upon entering the classroom, students read the Caught'ya, identify the problems, and write the passage as correctly as they can in a section of their notebooks labeled "Caught'yas."

Within a week of using this system, no directions are necessary! Students quickly get into the habit of entering the classroom and immediately getting to work on the Caught'ya. This solves the "getting settled" problem with loquacious students.

Students use one sheet of paper for each week's worth of Caught'yas. Students enter the classroom, look at the blackboard, get out the paper of that week's Caught'yas, and begin. First, they write correctly whatever day of the week it is. Even some of my advanced eighth graders misspell Wednesday, so this is my sneaky way of making them practice writing the days of the week. I usually put the day of the week on the board to identify the day's Caught'ya. I know this is not a good spelling practice, but I spell the day incorrectly and never capitalize it. Not only does this serve to identify the day's sentence and to practice writing the days of the week, but it also gives me a chance in STEP 7 to call on my weaker students to spell the day of the week, giving them some success. These students may not be able to identify comma errors, but they usually can spell the days of the week!

The minute the bell rings, I go over the meaning of the daily vocabulary word and give a dramatic reading of the Caught'ya. I often begin a quick discussion of whether that day's Caught'ya should begin a new paragraph and why. Sometimes, especially with my regular classes, I like to whisper a *sotto voce* warning that some error in the previous day's Caught'ya has been repeated in this one. My students love the drama.

Before I supply the meaning of the vocabulary word, I always try to elicit the meaning with theatrics. My students laugh at this, but it makes the Caught'ya more fun to do. I promised you grammar with a giggle, and this is the point where you have to begin laughing and hamming it up.

About once a week, after I go over the vocabulary word and read the Caught'ya, I like to have a quick plot discussion. This helps teach students to summarize. It also helps those students who have been absent to keep abreast of the plot. A quick values discussion also can result from this. "How must Gerald feel to be called a nerd?" "What do you think Hairy should do?" "Should Juliet run away? What could be the results?" Since the stories are geared to student interest, problems that worry students should be reflected in them.

Again I stress, students must keep all the Caught'yas for the entire week on the same sheet of paper. This is extremely important. If your students do not do this, you will be juggling too many papers each week when you grade the Caught'yas (Chapter 3). It also forces disorganized students to keep track of a piece of paper for one week. If you place great importance on this paper, even the most disorganized student eventually will get the idea.

It is important to introduce your daily sentence with enthusiasm. Your enthusiasm will engender your students' enthusiasm. You want to create a positive, fun atmosphere to surround this daily grammar exercise. Those of us who have used the Caught'ya system for years have found that the more humor and excitement we can attach to the daily sentence, the more successful the system is and the harder the students try to get the sentence correct.

Now that you have gone over the vocabulary word, have read the sentence dramatically, had any important discussions about paragraphing or about some value decision, and (assuming it is not a Monday) reminded your students to put the day's Caught'ya on the same sheet of paper as the previous day's Caught'ya, your students should try to write the daily sentence as correctly as they possibly can. I encourage my students who write or work more slowly to begin before the bell, so they will have a chance to finish with the rest of the class. My faster students also like to begin before the bell because they can't wait to be checked. This leads us to STEP 6.

Ten Easy Steps to a Successful Caught'ya

1. Outline or choose story plot.

2. Decide on skills and vocabulary word.

3. Compose daily sentence.

4. Write sentence incorrectly on board or overhead.

5. Students write Caught'ya as correctly as they can.

6. **Walk around, commenting on students' Caught'yas.**

7. Go to board and check Caught'ya with class.

8. Students mark mistakes with proofreading symbols.

9. Students count and indicate number of errors.

10. Collect Caught'yas at end of week.

STEP 6

 While the students attempt to write the Caught'ya sentence as correctly as they can, you circulate, offering individual encouragement, issuing challenges, goading students good-naturedly, or providing a quick mini-lesson in the grammar taught or reviewed in the sentence.

This is the point where the ham in you needs to surface. This is the step about which my students (when I asked them for advice to give in this book) were most vocal.

They told me to say that the more teasing, challenging, and poking that goes on while they are working on the Caught'ya, the more they love doing it. They also prefer it if you can briefly check the sentence of *every* child in the class to see whether you "caught 'im." They love this daily, humorous, individual contact.

While your students are working on the sentence, you walk around the room. In smaller classes I can get to every student. In larger classes of thirty or more, I usually get to half the class one day and the other half the next day. My students, however, do not like this; they insist that no matter how large the class, I should check everyone's Caught'ya. If time permits, and/or your students are willing to sit quietly and wait, it is probably worth the extra five minutes to look at every paper.

I briefly glance at a student's sentence to see if he/she found all the errors, to see if I "caught 'im." They love this! When I look at a student's sentence and I find that I didn't "catch 'im," I make a big deal of it, announcing to the class that so and so fooled me that day. I then say something to the effect that if a student didn't make any errors today, he or she is bound to make some tomorrow. I dare the student to get it right the next day. This encourages students to work harder the next day so that they can "best" me again. I often hear whispered arguments about the placement of a comma, paragraphing, or whatever error is in the sentence. This good-natured ribbing on my part really seems to make my students want to get the Caught'ya correct.

On the other hand, as is more usually the case, when I find an error the student didn't catch, I gently poke the student on the arm or make a funny face and say, "Caught'ya." The usual student response to this is to ask me where the error is located. Whether I identify the error depends on the student and the nature of the error.

If it is an error that I feel the student can correct without help, I shake my head and refuse to identify the line where the error is located, or to say how many errors I see. I challenge the student to find the error, and I make light of my refusal. Most students can't stand this, and before I can even move on to the next student, the previous student whom I "caught" is pouring over the sentence to find the error.

If, on the other hand, I feel that the error or errors are too difficult for a particular child to find, I usually try to give gentle hints. "What does a sentence always start with?" If I feel the student needs more than that, I give a quick mini-lesson in the skill. On the student's paper I mark in the correction and explain it. I then challenge the student to find this error on his own the next time, encouraging him to believe that he can. "I bet I won't catch you in that mistake again!" I often say.

I don't see the entire sentence of most of the children since I am circulating while they are working on it. Sometimes, even in my large classes, I quickly run around the room and look for one specific error. I sometimes challenge the class. "I'll catch every single one of you today. Heh. Heh. Heh." At that point, a little evil laughter spurs my students on to find that elusive and difficult error. Some run for the dictionaries. Others consult each other to try to prove me wrong. They love the friendly challenge.

After you have given your students the feedback on their work, you are ready to go over the Caught'ya with the whole class. Still issuing challenges or offering friendly encouragement, you saunter to the Caught'ya board and go on to STEP 7.

I must add a time saving postscript at this point. If you wish, while you are running around the room checking to see which of your students you "caught," you can also make a quick homework check! I first take roll and mark in the absentees, then I instruct the students to place their homework in a visible place on their desks. As I cavort around the room, gradebook in hand, I easily notice those students who do not have their homework. I immediately mark a zero in my gradebook for that child's homework and continue around the room, checking Caught'yas and homework.

When I have a few seconds sometime later in the period, I mark in the checks for those students who had their homework. I only mark the zeros as I walk around since there are fewer of them than checks. Since I grade homework for completion, not correctness, this works well. It also smooths the transition to checking the homework after you have completed the Caught'ya.

Ten Easy Steps to a Successful Caught'ya

1. Outline or choose story plot.

2. Decide on skills and vocabulary word.

3. Compose daily sentence.

4. Write sentence incorrectly on board or overhead.

5. Students write Caught'ya as correctly as they can.

6. Walk around, commenting on students' Caught'yas.

7. **Go to board and check Caught'ya with class.**

8. Students mark mistakes with proofreading symbols.

9. Students count and indicate number of errors.

10. Collect Caught'yas at end of week.

STEP 7

 After your students have written the sentence as correctly as they can and you have given them your animated feedback, return to the blackboard or overhead and elicit the corrections from the class.

Now that your students have written the Caught'ya sentence as correctly as they can and you have cavorted around the classroom checking to see whom you "caught," it is time to check the Caught'ya. This is a serious procedure interspersed with explanations of grammar.

Elicit the errors from your students. Ask them what is wrong with the Caught'ya. When they tell you what is wrong, press further and insist on an explanation of why the correction needs to be made. After a few months of this, students usually can recite correctly, for example, why a comma should go in a particular place, the part of speech of any given word, whether there should be a paragraph, whether the tense of the verb is correct, whether the subject agrees with the verb, etc., etc.. You can include spelling rules, punctuation, irregular verbs, or anything you desire. *The "why" is just as important as the correction.*

Your students should visualize as well as hear the corrections so correct the Caught'ya on the board or overhead in a different color chalk or overhead pen. Use proofreading symbols to mark the errors. These proofreading symbols should be prominently displayed on the wall near the spot where you locate the Caught'ya. (See STEP 8 for a sample of the proofreading symbols you might want to use.)

Instruct your students to find the errors they missed the first time when they wrote the Caught'ya themselves. When they find an error they missed, they are to use the appropriate proofreading symbol to correct it and then write in the correction. For example, if a word is spelled wrong, a student should circle the word, put "sp." to indicate the error, and then write the word correctly above the misspelled word. If any punctuation has been forgotten, the spot should be circled and the proper punctuation put inside the circle. If any extra punctuation has been included, or a letter capitalized that should not have been, it should be circled (to make it easier to see) and marked through with the "delete" symbol. The correction, if any, should be written above the circle.

All of these marks *should be done in a different color* from that of the Caught'ya. This makes it easier for a student to see his errors for future reference. Since you repeat the same mistakes over and over in subsequent Caught'ya sentences, students can avoid repeating the same error. Another reason to mark errors in another color is to make it easier for you to grade the Caught'ya. I usually subtract five points from the score of any student who doesn't correct the sentence in a different color. See the Caught'ya evaluation procedure in Chapter 3.

This method corrects the errors missed the first time the student copied the sentence. It has three purposes. One, it teaches editing. Two, it teaches the proofreading symbols. Three, it makes the Caught'yas a positive experience for even your lowest student. Since you grade the Caught'yas on whether the students caught the errors the *second* time (when you went over them on the board, writing in the corrections so that the students could copy these corrections onto their own papers), even your slowest student can experience success.

If students pay attention, each of them can earn an A+ grade. Your quicker students won't make so many mistakes the first time when they correct the Caught'ya on their own. Your less skilled students will miss more the first time, but still can get the same grade as the quicker students if they pay attention and write in the corrections the second time. This feeling of success for ALL students is one of the things that makes the Caught'yas so popular with students. Everyone, not just the best students, can earn an A+.

Before we go on to STEP 8, let me emphasize again the importance of going over the "why" of a correction. The students hear the explanation in context and can readily learn a grammar, mechanics, or usage rule. Students like to know why they are doing something. If they understand why, they tend to carry the correct English to their own writing.

Ten Easy Steps to a Successful Caught'ya

1. Outline or choose story plot.

2. Decide on skills and vocabulary word.

3. Compose daily sentence.

4. Write sentence incorrectly on board or overhead.

5. Students write Caught'ya as correctly as they can.

6. Walk around, commenting on students' Caught'yas.

7. Go to board and check Caught'ya with class.

8. **Students mark mistakes with proofreading symbols.**

9. Students count and indicate number of errors.

10. Collect Caught'yas at end of week.

STEP 8

 During the group correction of the Caught'ya, instruct your students to use proofreading symbols to mark the corrections on their Caught'yas. These marks should be made clearly with a colored pencil, pen, or marker. In addition, for study purposes, students should write out the corrections.

As I mentioned in STEP 7, students should use proof-reading symbols to mark the errors on the Caught'ya when you go over the sentence as a group. These symbols mark the errors that the students did not catch the first time when they tried to write the Caught'ya sentence as correctly as they could on their own.

Obviously the lower the grade level, the simpler the proofreading marks you will want to use. Look at the grammar book you use for your grade. There is always a page of proofreading symbols suggested for use at that grade level. Even a third grader can use three lines under a letter not capitalized or circle a spot where punctuation is needed.

In this section, I have included some of the proofreading marks you might want to use. These are just suggestions. It is imperative, though, that you decide which symbols you wish to teach and make a poster of those symbols. This poster should be put somewhere near the spot where you write the daily Caught'ya sentence. Students do refer to the chart often.

By using these symbols all year, students become familiar with them. I have noticed that, by the second half of the year, they unconsciously use these symbols to correct their own written work when they edit.

Again, students are to correct their sentences in another color so that they can clearly see the errors they were unable to notice the first time around. This provides them with a study tool and a reference so that future mistakes of the same nature can be avoided.

Suggested Proofreading Symbols

⌗ = indent

⌗ = take out indent

∧ = add words here

○ = add punctuation
(Whatever is
inside circle.)

℮ = take out

$\underset{=}{a}$ = capitalize

A̸ = make a small letter

→ = move word

ⓐⓝⓓ = reverse order

Ten Easy Steps to a Successful Caught'ya

1. Outline or choose story plot.

2. Decide on skills and vocabulary word.

3. Compose daily sentence.

4. Write sentence incorrectly on board or overhead.

5. Students write Caught'ya as correctly as they can.

6. Walk around, commenting on students' Caught'yas.

7. Go to board and check Caught'ya with class.

8. Students mark mistakes with proofreading symbols.

9. **Students count and indicate number of errors.**

10. Collect Caught'yas at end of week.

STEP 9

 Instruct your students to count the errors that they did not correct the first time around on their own. Instruct them also to write this number in the margin beside the Caught'ya sentence.

This step doesn't need much more explanation. The grade on the Caught'ya has nothing to do with the errors that a student missed when he attempted to write the sentence correctly on his own. The grade will depend on whether the error was caught the second time when the Caught'ya sentence was corrected with the class. A student can miss *every* error the first time and still earn an A+ if the errors are caught and clearly marked as errors when you go over the Caught'ya as a class.

Students write the number of errors they did not catch the first time around to provide you with an easy method of grading the Caught'yas. This also forces them to use margins. It has the added advantage of giving you a quick diagnosis as to whether your students are learning a skill. It provides your students with feedback on their improvement. You and your students will discover that the errors become fewer and fewer as the year wears on.

Some students are not happy to admit error and will be tempted just to quietly make the corrections without marking them as errors missed. Encourage, cajole, forbid, threaten, do anything to discourage this.

I even tell my students that if they never miss anything on these Caught'yas, they had better get an A+ on all their grammar tests. I also threaten (and follow through and do it) to go back and give zeros on previous Caught'yas if a student has rarely missed anything in the Caught'yas and shows me, either in writing or in a test, that the skill has not been mastered. Students catch on quickly that by cheating and not marking errors, they only hurt themselves in the long run. This, in itself, is a great lesson.

Ten Easy Steps to a Successful Caught'ya

1. Outline or choose story plot.

2. Decide on skills and vocabulary word.

3. Compose daily sentence.

4. Write sentence incorrectly on board or overhead.

5. Students write Caught'ya as correctly as they can.

6. Walk around, commenting on students' Caught'yas.

7. Go to board and check Caught'ya with class.

8. Students mark mistakes with proofreading symbols.

9. Students count and indicate number of errors.

10. **Collect Caught'yas at end of week.**

STEP 10

 Instruct your students to draw a line under the day's Caught'ya sentence. The next day's Caught'ya will be written underneath. All the Caught'yas for the week are to be put on the same piece of paper. Students who have been absent simply write the day they missed and the word "absent" in the blank space.

It is important that all the Caught'yas for one week go on the same sheet of paper. This makes it easier for you to grade the papers since you have only one per student. It also helps the students see what has gone on before. I often work on the same skill for a week and keep repeating errors in that skill in subsequent Caught'yas. If all the Caught'yas for the week are on the same page, then students readily can see what corrections need to be made. It also makes it easier to discover whether or not a new paragraph needs to be started.

I always begin the period with a dramatic reading of the day's Caught'ya, a definition of the vocabulary word, and a discussion of whether or not the sentence begins a new paragraph. I instruct students to look over the previous Caught'yas for that week and to decide whether a new paragraph is necessary. They become adept at this rather quickly. I have found that this paragraphing does carry over into their writing. My students write a weekly journal. After a few months of the school year have passed, I always notice that paragraphing starts to appear, without any suggestion from me! If students are required to think about paragraphing four or five times a week for thirty-six weeks, it usually becomes habit.

When I grade the Caught'yas, I subtract ten points if all the Caught'yas for that week are not on the same page. It is surprising how even the messiest child learns to hang onto that piece of paper. Since Caught'yas are 1/8th of their final grade, my students value that piece of paper!

At the end of the week, collect the Caught'yas from your students. Every time I collect the Caught'yas, I usually remind the students to write their names, the date (writing out the month for spelling practice), and the word "Caught'ya." I am very picky about the format for the paper and margins. My students quickly learn to check their Caught'ya papers very carefully before handing them to me for grading.

Since Caught'yas are a classroom activity only, it is impossible for absent students to make them up. Simply instruct any student who was absent the day of a Caught'ya to leave a blank space for that day on the weekly Caught'ya sheet. In that space, instruct them to write in the day missed and the word "absent." When you grade the Caught'yas, you easily can check up on a student you suspect was not absent. This practice makes the

Caught'yas even more pleasant for your students since they do not have them hanging over their heads to make up if they miss a day. My students tell me that they appreciate this. A few missed Caught'yas won't hurt, and the good will it generates is worth it.

Now that you have read the ten steps to the Caught'ya, you need to know how to evaluate them.

Lesson Plans for the Caught'ya

NOTE: These plans assume that you have already completed Steps 1, 2, and 3, that your story and sentences are ready, or that you plan to use my already prepared Caught'ya sentences in Chapters 6, 7, or 8.

- Before school, write the daily sentence on the board, box the vocabulary word, and indicate the number of errors below the sentence if you wish.

- As students enter the classroom, instruct them to copy the sentence as correctly as they can.

- Read the sentence to the class with a dramatic flair, reviewing the story, going over the meaning of the vocabulary word, and discussing whether the sentence begins a paragraph.

- Walk around the room, giving students individual feedback. Say "Caught'ya" if you catch a student with an error and praise or challenge a student who has caught all the errors. Remember, students will not have finished the sentence by the time you get to them. Just look at what they have.

- Go back to the blackboard or overhead and check the Caught'ya sentence out loud with your class. Elicit answers from your students. Be sure to discuss the reason for each correction. Correct the Caught'ya on the board or overhead by using proofreading symbols. Instruct students to do the same on their papers.

- Instruct students to count their errors and indicate them in the right margin. Instruct them to mark a line under the Caught'ya to separate it from the next day's Caught'ya. If it is the last Caught'ya of the week, collect each student's paper.

How to Evaluate the Caught'ya

The evaluation of the Caught'yas is just as important as the process of doing them. Caught'yas can eliminate the feeling of failure on the part of your students. Students who had long ago given up hope of any success in language arts begin to try again because they know that they now can succeed. Even your worst student can earn an A+ week after week on his Caught'yas. How? The Caught'yas are graded *not* on how well a student initially grasps the English language, but on how carefully that student corrected the grammar when you and the class went over the Caught'ya at the blackboard or on the overhead.

This is very important to remember! Caught'yas are not graded conventionally. You are not grading the English or the lack of it in the traditional manner. You base grades on whether or not your students *caught* the errors. In this way, a student who repeatedly catches all the errors on his own the first time around gets the same grade as a student who made twenty errors the first time around, *as long as the student who made the twenty errors caught every one of those errors and marked them correctly* when the class went over the Caught'ya. By modeling the corrections on the blackboard or overhead, you make it easy for *every* student to succeed with the Caught'yas.

While some of you may have trouble with this method of grading, keep in mind that your goal is the end result, not the immediate grade. Encouraged by good grades and by the individual, daily feedback, your students who are weak in grammar often are inspired to achieve near-miracles of improvement in their writing.

I have taught fifth, seventh, and eighth graders who, at the beginning of the year, never began a sentence with a capital letter, let alone put any punctuation at the end. These same students (remember Stephanie in Chapter 1?) are often the ones who become the quickest to recite and identify the prepositions, or the coordinating conjunctions, or to point out that a comma must be placed in a compound sentence, or to notice that a series needs commas. They become infused with their success and with their knowledge of the correct answers. They are the first to raise their hands when the class goes over the Caught'ya. They *know* they have the right answer.

The result in their writing is magic. I have to smile sometimes to see the periods and commas in these students' papers written much larger than normal. They want me to notice their prowess! While these students often don't master the more sophisticated art of the semicolon, or the elimination of dangling modifiers, or the use of correct verb tense, they do manage consistently to punctuate a quotation, or use commas correctly, and of course, begin sentences with capital letters and end them with the appropriate punctuation.

Success with the Caught'yas is good for student morale. A happy student *does* try harder. The more careful your students are in their proofreading efforts, the fewer errors they make. My weaker students often do better than my advanced ones. Success in language arts is new to them. They are willing to work for it! Please keep this in mind when you grade the Caught'yas.

Following the principle that any at-home paper grading time should be spent reading my students' writing efforts as opposed to correcting grammar assignments (including Caught'yas), I have tried to reduce the Caught'ya correcting time to a minimum. This has been a communal effort with several fellow teachers over a number of years. All of us are dedicated to the idea of spending more time with our families and hobbies and less time with the rote part of our school work. The result is a simple, efficient way to grade the Caught'yas that takes about ten minutes a week for a class of thirty students!

I promised you "grammar with a giggle." Now is the time you get to giggle to yourself as you reduce the grammar grading time to a mere ten minutes or less per class per week. There are, however, several things on which you must be certain to insist in your classes on the days that you do the Caught'yas.

On Friday, or any day you prefer, collect your students' Caught'yas for the week. As I suggested in Chapter 2, insist that your students put all of their Caught'ya sentences for one week on the same sheet of paper. I even go so far as to subtract ten points from the grade of the week's Caught'yas if a student has used more than one sheet of paper for the week. Having only one sheet of paper per student greatly reduces paper shuffling time. It also makes it easier to return the graded papers. I am obnoxiously strict about the one-paper-per-week rule. My students sense that I am very serious about this and often hang on to their Caught'ya papers above all others.

When doing the Caught'yas, you also have to decide on the paper format that is important to you. Over the years, I have found that the following picky points work well. Insist on a student's full name in the upper right-hand corner of the paper with the date of the first Caught'ya of the week written out underneath. I also force my students to write out the day of the week for each Caught'ya. This gives them vital spelling practice. Insist on no abbreviations for the month because writing out the month is especially good practice for those months like February that are difficult to spell.

There is always a purpose for my madness and a reason for my pickiness. Whether or not students complain, I always explain why I demand these picky things on their papers. It helps my students' attitudes. An easy way to make your point is to ask your students to write the word "Wednesday" on a piece of paper. Many (including half of your advanced students) will, of course, misspell it. This will make your point more graphically than any other way.

After I make my point with the word "Wednesday," I always whisper to my students the embarrassing fact that I misspelled the word "forty" for the first thirty years of my life. I also tell them that if they let this secret out, I will publicize *their* egregious spelling errors. Remember that cooperation and shared secrets are important for the overall success of the Caught'yas.

On the first line of the paper I require a title. This is the word "Caught'ya." I require this because my middle school students often have a difficult time remembering to capitalize the first letter of words (except prepositions and noun markers) in titles. This gives them practice.

I also stress margins. Students often forget the boundaries of their papers. It is important to make them aware of margins. What better place to be strict about margins than in a paper that is handed in once a week for every week of school? By the end of the year *all* of my students leave appropriate margins on all of their papers!

Of course, you can stress whatever format or form is important to you. It does not matter. You even may want to come up with a three-word title for more title practice. I remind my students of my required format *every* week. I also remind them that I take off ten points per error in the format.

Every time your students complete a Caught'ya, it is imperative to point out that they should indicate the number of errors they do not catch in the sentence the first time around. They should write this number in the right-hand margin next to the appropriate Caught'ya and circle it to make it easier for you to read.

Finally, emphasize to your students that they must mark their corrections and indicate the number missed *in a different color* from the one in which the Caught'ya is written. This makes your grading job much easier. It also makes the Caught'yas a study tool for your students since they can see their errors more easily.

I also need to warn you to get out your colored pens. Since your students use two colors on their papers, you will have to use a third color to correct them. I usually correct my students' papers in green. They rarely use green pens, and green is such a positive color. I never correct in red since I am trying to get away from all the traditional trappings that have given language arts a bad taste in the mouths of many students.

Now that you have insisted on the correct format, have collected the papers, and have colored pen in hand, you are ready to grade the Caught'yas. For painless grading and happy students, follow the three simple steps explained in the following pages.

These steps assume that you have a paper in front of you. I have tried to give you examples at the end of each step. If you need more visual help, look at the sample student papers at the end of this chapter.

Basic Format Rules for Easy Caught'ya Grading

Tell your students to:

- Put all Caught'yas for the week on the same piece of paper.

- Write full name on the paper wherever you decide you want it.

- Write out the full date of the first Caught'ya of the week, including spelling out the month. Put this underneath the name.

- Write a title on the first line of the paper. The word "Caught'ya" is fine.

- Spell out the day of the week above the Caught'ya for that day.

- Indicate the number of missed errors to the right of each Caught'ya.

- Mark errors in a color different from that of the sentence.

- Be careful to leave margins.

STEP 1: Check Format

Glance at the paper first. Has the student put all the Caught'yas for the week on the same sheet of paper? Next, check to see that the format you insisted on has been correctly executed. Check for the student's name and the date of the first Caught'ya of the week underneath it. Is the child's name capitalized? Is the month and are the days of the week spelled correctly and capitalized? Is there a comma in the correct place in the date? Next, check the title. Is it correct? Have the days of the week been spelled correctly and capitalized? Has the student indicated the number wrong for each sentence? Are the errors marked in a different color? Are the margins relatively straight, and are they large enough?

If any of these things is incorrect, circle it, indicate what is wrong, and put a -10 beside it. I usually only take off five points for each side of the margin and five points if two colors have not been used but ten points for everything else. If a student is exceptionally careless (usually this happens only a few times in the beginning of the year), then all one hundred points could be lost on the format alone!

Things to Look for:

- Name written correctly. -10

- Date written out correctly underneath, month spelled out completely. -10

- Title correctly written and capitalized. -10

- Days of the week correctly spelled above each sentence. -10

- Number of uncaught errors indicated and circled to the right of each Caught'ya. -10 each

- Errors corrected in another color. -5

- Margins fairly even. -5 each margin

- All Caught'yas for the week on the same sheet of paper. -10

Two sample student papers follow. Please note that on the first paper Stephanie has indicated correctly that she was absent one day. She lost ten points because she failed to capitalize October. She lost another ten points for forgetting to indicate the number wrong in Tuesday's Caught'ya. She lost another ten points for misspelling Wednesday. If she made no more errors in correcting her Caught'yas, then her grade would be a seventy. Stephanie, who was one of my seventh grade students, learned quickly. By November, she no longer made these obvious errors in her papers.

On the second paper Sylvia, another former student, carefully and correctly followed the format. If she had corrected all her errors on the sentences, she would have earned a one hundred on her paper!

Stephanie's Caught'yas are a part of the Hairy Beast story that you will find in Chapter 7. Sylvia's Caught'yas come from sentences made from the fourth story idea suggested in Chapter 5 entitled "_____ Mean School."

(70)

Careful, Stephanie, these are errors you know how to avoid. Mrs. K.

-10

Stephanie
October 24, 1989

NOTE:
Student wrote word "absent" when she missed class.

Caught'ya

Monday

→ABSENT

Tuesday

Wilfred wrote Hairy the pompous note and Bertha sent him flowers.

Put # wrong! -10

-10 sp.

Wednesday

When the doorbell rang, Hairy hoping it was news from Hilda crept out of his hiding place in the bathtub and agitatedly answered the door.

-3

Thursday

He adored the flowers from Bertha but he was insulted by Hairy's inadvertently unkind note.

-2

Friday

Hairy felt overwhelmed. He had been jilted by his girl, insulted by his friend, and had his warts vilified.

-1

Format wrong. -20
I checked Wednesday's Caughtya. -10

Regular 7th grade student.

90

Caught'ya (Small **H!**)

Sylvia
5 period
January 21, 1987

Wednesday (-O) → ⊖
Locker Larry caught J.J. and Sam in the ⊗l and said, "Maybe if we take a picture of May Bellina and leave it lying around..."

Thursday (-O)
"...so she will ①clearly see how she looks. This might make her ②quickly realize how her appearance has changed ③for the worse since she started hanging ④out with that ⑤very made-up Este Lauder."

Friday (-2)
The group (carefully) chose a land-mark as a background and started taking pictures. Sam took the film home to develop (more) (quickly.) Sam isn't [lax.]

Good work, Sylvia!
Watch those extra capital letters...
Mrs. K.

Format O.K.
I checked the first one. -10

Regular 7th grade student.

STEP 2: Check Content of One Caught'ya

Choose *one* of the week's Caught'yas. This is where you will save the most time. I assure you that if you read all of the sentences for each of your students, the final grade would be about the same as if you read only one.

My fellow teachers and I have experimented for years with this. When I first invented the idea of the Caught'ya and implemented it in my classroom, I carefully read every sentence that my students wrote. This got to be a real chore each week. I knew that the idea was great, but if there was no efficient way to grade the papers, it wasn't practical.

I struggled for about two years, reading every Caught'ya. I then began to notice that if I increased the number of points per error and graded only *one* Caught'ya per student, the grade almost always came out the same. Other teachers independently came to the same conclusion. We conferred, pooled our guilt at not reading every sentence that our students wrote, and threw it out our classroom windows.

Since students don't know which sentence you plan to check, they tend to be careful on all the sentences. If you read only one sentence per child, you quickly memorize that sentence as you grade. That reduces grading time even more.

I know it will be hard for some of you to accept, as it was for me, but you really waste your time reading all the sentences. Reading one for evaluation *is* just as effective. Since it reduces your grading time by a factor of three or four depending on how many Caught'yas you choose to do per week, it is essential.

To tell the truth, every once in a while when I have a free weekend, I'll read all the sentences on my students' papers. Every time I do this, I am amazed that the grades that I enter into my gradebook for each child do not vary much from previous grades. Since you are really checking for carefulness, a spot check of one Caught'ya per week suffices to give a grade and to keep your students honest.

Now that you are convinced, hopefully, to grade only one of the Caught'yas, you need to know what to do with that one sentence. Since you are grading only one, you can grade it carefully.

Read the Caught'ya. Did the student write the Caught'ya correctly the first time when you went around the room poking shoulders and announcing which students did not make an error? If not, did the student clearly mark the errors made in the proofreading symbols you want him to use? Did he make the correction above the marked errors? Did he catch *every* error either the first time or the second time? Did he count up the number of errors correctly and indicate that number in the margin to the side of the Caught'ya? Did the student make these corrections in another color from that of the sentence itself? Did the student spell all the words correctly? Did he copy the sentence correctly from the board? Are there any extraneous capital letters?

Take ten points off for every error not caught, not marked, or the correction not written in above the marked error. Take ten points off for any error added in because of copying the sentence incorrectly, words missed, etc. Each tiny error is worth ten points.

I feel that this is not too much to deduct for each error. First of all, you are grading only one sentence. Second, the student merely had to copy the corrections correctly from the blackboard or overhead when you went over the Caught'ya with the class. You are grading your students on how well they noted the corrected English, not on how good their initial efforts were. This is why students feel so good about the Caught'yas.

As I have indicated above, students who had never before experienced success in language arts classes now can achieve that success. Laurel Harb, a fellow teacher of mine, tried the Caught'yas on her compensatory class. The results were astounding. The students learned to proofread. They began to write more correctly. They looked forward to language arts. They were very careful to mark all their errors because they wanted that A+ on their Caught'ya paper each week. The end result of the class was that almost half of her students tested out of compensatory language arts that spring! Laurel vows that if ever she teaches another compensatory class, she will use the Caught'yas. She also, by the way, has used Caught'yas in her regular and advanced English classes for four years.

Speaking of advanced or accelerated students, at first they sometimes try to maintain an aloof attitude concerning the

Caught'yas. They often feel as if they know it all. They too, however, soon fall under the spell of the amusing stories and are humbled by mistakes they make when they first write the Caught'ya on their own. Even more than regular or compensatory students, advanced students feel very strongly that they do not wish to be caught by their teacher. Parents have told me that their children will study grammar and usage rules just so I won't "catch 'em" on their Caught'yas. I often see my advanced students clustered around the Caught'ya board before class begins, debating corrections for the sentence.

Things to Look for When Grading Caught'ya Content:

- All errors either written correctly by the student or caught and marked with proofreaders' marks.
- All corrections written in above the marked errors.
- Errors marked in a different color from the sentence.
- No words written incorrectly.
- No extraneous capital letters.
- No words skipped or substituted.

On the next page are five students' versions of a single Caught'ya. Note how the errors are marked. Assume that the format was correct on the rest of each of these papers. I have indicated each student's grade to the left of each Caught'ya. Note also that since I grade only one sentence per week, I can afford the time to make brief comments on my students' papers. This continues the one-on-one contact that helps make the Caught'yas so popular.

Because these examples are only in one color, the teacher's marks are indicated by solid black lines. The student examples are represented in grey. On the original papers there were three colors — one for the original attempt at the Caught'ya, another for the student's corrections when we went over the Caught'ya at the blackboard, and the third for my marks and comments. This Caught'ya sentence comes from the revised *Romeo and Juliet* story in Chapter 8.

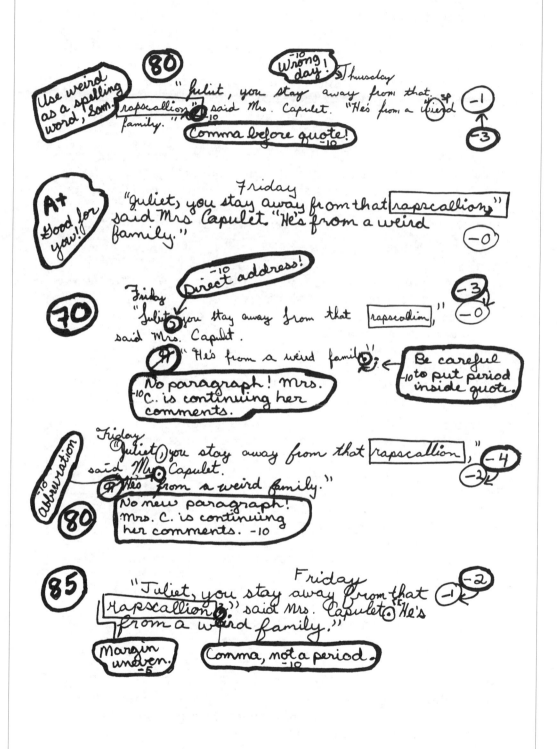

Use weird as a spelling word, Sam.

80

Wrong! day! -10 S Thursday

"Juliet, you stay away from that sp rapscallion," said Mrs. Capulet. "He's from a weird family." -1 ↑ -3

Comma before quote! -10

A+ Good for you!

Friday

"Juliet, you stay away from that rapscallion," said Mrs. Capulet. "He's from a weird family." -0

70

Friday Direct address! -10

"Juliet, you stay away from that rapscallion," said Mrs. Capulet. -3 -0

¶ "He's from a weird family." Be careful -10 to put period inside quote.

No paragraph! Mrs. C. is continuing her comments.

80

To Abbreviation

Friday

"Juliet, you stay away from that rapscallion," said Mrs. Capulet. -4 -2

¶ He's from a weird family."

No new paragraph! Mrs. C. is continuing her comments. -10

85

Friday

"Juliet, you stay away from that rapscallion," said Mrs. Capulet. "He's from a weird family." -1 -2

Margin uneven. -5

Comma, not a period. -10

STEP 3: Reward the Students

I pass the papers back to my students. I instruct them to look at where they failed to catch the errors. Since most of the mistakes tend to be a result of carelessness, students are very serious about noting the errors. As stated in STEP 2, *all* of my students know that they can get an A+ on their Caught'ya paper if they take care. Most of them do look at their mistakes so that they won't repeat them the next time.

Before I used the Caught'ya system of teaching grammar, I often felt that all my careful, time-consuming work of marking errors on students' papers was in vain. With the Caught'yas, students take their few mistakes seriously since they know that they can prevent these errors the next time.

I carry the encouragement and feeling of success one step further. I reward the students who receive an A+ for the week on their Caught'yas. Since lotteries are the "in" thing in many states nowadays, I give half of a 3 x 5 file card to each student who earns an A+ on his or her Caught'yas for the week. The student writes name, class period, and the date on the card. The proud student then gets up and ostentatiously puts the card in a "lottery" box I have on a table in my room. This card is that student's ticket to my Caught'ya lottery.

Twice a year I open the box (I put a piece of construction paper over the bottom) and take out a card. If it is the card of a student in that class, I award the child a prize: a small stuffed animal, a candy bar, etc. If the card belongs to a student in another class, I put it back and keep drawing until I get a card of someone in that specific class. I repeat this every period of the day so that there is a winner in each of my language arts classes. Parents, delighted with the system, now happily donate many of the prizes; hence, I am not out of pocket so much these days. Even if you pay for the prizes yourself, it is well worth the expense. Students will give an extra measure of care to earn that lottery ticket.

The Caught'ya lottery is an easy, painless, no-work-for-you way to reward and encourage your students. You would be convinced to try it if you could just once see one of my slower students prance up to the box, prominently displaying his card. Not only do these students have the reward of winning the ticket and possibly winning the prize, but they *publicly* get to advertise their success in front of the entire class when they march up to the box to insert their ticket. It is a moment of sweet triumph for some students who do not experience much success elsewhere in their lives!

Sample Caught'ya Papers

The following three sample Caught'ya papers were taken from the same class. Two of them are from the same week; the third is from another week. The Caught'ya story is the one found in Chapter 8, based on Shakespeare's *Romeo and Juliet*. Again, please note that each original paper contained three colors, two from the student and one from me. For clarity, my marks and remarks are indicated by solid black lines. Students' examples are represented in grey.

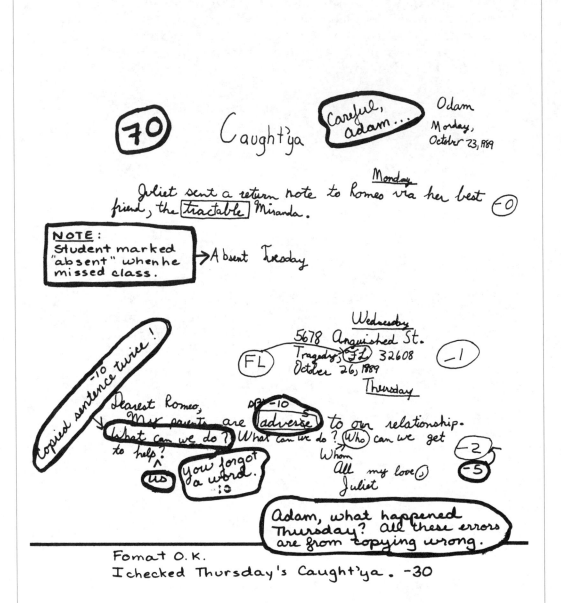

70 Caught'ya — *Careful, adam...*

Odam
Monday,
October 23, 1989

Monday
Juliet sent a return note to Romeo via her best friend, the ~tractable~ Miranda. — -0

NOTE: Student marked "absent" when he missed class. → Absent Tuesday

Wednesday
5678 Anguished St. — FL
Tragedy, FL 32608 — -1
October 26, 1989

Thursday

Dearest Romeo,
~My parents~ are ~adverse~ to our relationship. — -10
What can we do? What can we do? Who can we get — -2
to help? Whom
us you forgot all my love☺ — -5
a word. :) Juliet

copied sentence twice! -10

Adam, what happened Thursday? All these errors are from copying wrong.

Fomat O.K.
I checked Thursday's Caught'ya. -30

Advanced 8th grade student.

90

Erin
November 6, 1989

Caught'ya

Group leader, absent — Monday

Note: My students needed more practice with who and whom, so I changed caught'ya #29 (see p. 189) to provide that extra practice.

Note:
Student marked "absent" because she was doing another assignment.

Tuesday
One day⊙ Romeo arrived at the mall's parking lot with his cousin, the quick⊖tempered Benvolio. He planned to ⌈amble⌉ through with Juliet, whom he adored. (-2)

Note:
I took nothing off as I checked Friday's Caught'ya.

Thursday
At the same time, Juliet's ⌈ingenious⌉ cousin Tybalt was arriving at the mall. The two cars crashed and a fight ⌈ensued⌉. (-3)

missed comma -10

Friday
"Tybalt, you low down ⌈cretin⌉ take that!" yelled Benvolio at Tybalt as he slugged the latter in the chest. (-0) ← (-1)

Format O.K.
I checked Friday's Caught'ya. -10
Note: Although Erin misspelled a word in Thursday's Caught'ya, it doesn't count against her because I only check one Caught'ya/week.

Advanced 8th grade student.

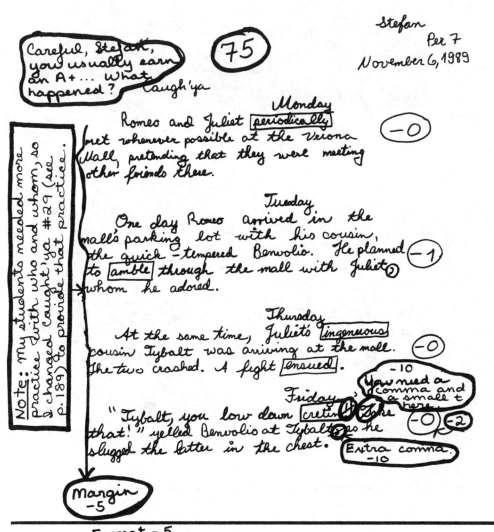

Careful, Stefan, you usually earn an A+... What happened? Caught'ya

75

Stefan
Per 7
November 6, 1989

Monday

Romeo and Juliet periodically met whenever possible at the Verona Mall, pretending that they were meeting other friends there.

−0

Tuesday

One day Romeo arrived in the mall's parking lot with his cousin, the quick-tempered Benvolio. He planned to amble through the mall with Juliet whom he adored.

−1

Thursday

At the same time, Juliet's ingenuous cousin Tybalt was arriving at the mall. The two crashed. A fight ensued.

−0

Friday

"Tybalt, you low down cretin take that!" yelled Benvolio at Tybalt as he slugged the latter in the chest.

You need a comma and a small t here. −10

−0 −2

Extra comma. −10

Note: My students needed more practice with who and whom, so I changed caught'ya #29 (see p. 189) to provide that practice.

Margin −5

Format. −5
I checked Friday's Caught'ya. −20

Advanced 8th grade student.

Practice Grading Sheet

Use the sample Caught'yas on the following page to practice grading the Caught'yas. This paper is an example of the typical errors that students of any grade level make. While you normally would correct only *one* Caught'ya on a student's paper, correct *all* of these for practice. On the succeeding page, I have reproduced the same sample paper with all the proper corrections. Corrections are noted in the left-hand margin.

Jane
July 31, 1989

Caught'ya Evaluation practice

Monday

(H) While Juliet's family was going nuts,
Juliet was truely (sp truly) languishing in the (-3)
tomb from the dearth of food.

Tuesday

She felt giddy and lightheaded, and
she finally droped off into a dreamless
sleep.

Wednesday

Romeo, not finding any transportation
except his own (2) two feet hoofed it (50) fifty
miles to the church.   — 3

Thursday

He trekked all threw (sp through) the night,   (-4)
and most of the day (next) berating his
himself the whole time for their
stupidity in fighting.

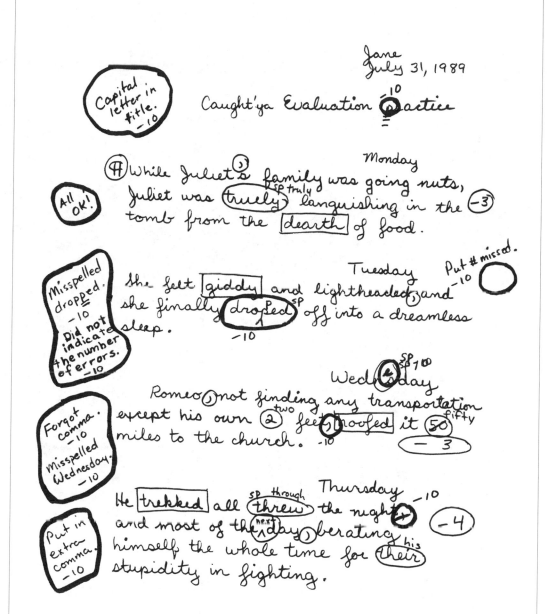

Jane
July 31, 1989

Caught'ya Evaluation Practice

Capital letter in title. -10

All OK!

Monday

While Juliet's family was going nuts, Juliet was (truely) languishing in the tomb from the [dearth] of food.   -3

sp truly

Tuesday

She felt [giddy] and lightheaded, and she finally (dropped) off into a dreamless sleep.   -10

Put # missed. -10

Misspelled dropped. -10
Did not indicate the number of errors. -10

Wednesday

Romeo not finding any transportation except his own (2) two feet (hoofed) it (50) fifty miles to the church.   -3   -10

Forgot comma. -10
Misspelled Wednesday. -10

Thursday

He [trekked] all (threw) the night and most of the (day) berating himself the whole time for (their) stupidity in fighting.   -10   -4

sp through   *next*   *his*

Put in extra comma. -10

Beyond the Basic Caught'ya

Vocabulary
Dreaded Spelling
Diagramming Sentences
Writing Assignments and Showing Writing
Tests
Hype

Now that you understand the basic Caught'ya technique, you are ready to take it a few steps further. You *never* want to spend more than five to ten minutes a day on the daily Caught'ya. If you linger over it or make it a much longer activity, then it becomes mundane and drawn out like this run on sentence, and you will lose your students' interest. How can you make the most of those eight minutes or so? Can you tantalize your students with more juicy tidbits of your Caught'ya story in other assignments without overdoing the concept? How can you further excite your students to enjoy learning English skills? Caught'yas can become the framework around which you can add other English skills like vocabulary enrichment, spelling, learning parts of speech, sentence diagramming, and most importantly, writing.

Vocabulary

Stress the vocabulary words you introduce in your Caught'yas and use them as often as you can in conversations with your students. Make sure to reinforce these words in an amusing, non-threatening manner that appeals to your students. It is easy to introduce a difficult word like "lugubrious" in a humorous fashion. After the word appears in the Caught'ya, use it frequently in your own speech.

For example, I have abandoned the use of the phrase "a lot" (students can never remember whether it is one word or two anyway) and have substituted "a plethora of" instead. Students mimic you very quickly. They love using words that their parents may not know. "What a lugubrious face you have today, Mary. What's wrong? Do you have a plethora of woes?" This is, of course, an exaggeration, but judicious and conscious use of these words in normal conversation is very effective. You develop a private language with your students. They love this feeling of a secret club.

Encourage your students to use these words in their writing for extra credit. Tell them to box the word the way you do in the daily Caught'ya. If the word is correctly used, add a point to the child's grade on the paper if you grade writing. If you don't put grades on student writing, you can keep a running tab of correctly used vocabulary words in your grade book. At the end of each grading period, tally the number of vocabulary words a student used correctly and add a point or two to the final grade for the marking period.

I also have found that students who are weaker in English skills love to try to use the longer words. It gives them a genuine feeling of accomplishment, and they have not expended much effort.

Below is a test of a seventh grade boy whose skills were very limited. The paper is a friendly letter format test in which the students were instructed to write a letter to the Caught'ya character Hairy Beast to console him for the recent loss of his girlfriend. Students were told to use their own addresses in the heading. You can see from Demetrius's grade that he is not a careful nor a superior student. He did, however, use the word "dulcet" correctly. He was so proud of using this word (and others in his other writing efforts) that I know he still uses them in his speech. He thinks it's "cool" to use these words!

-30 letter format
+- 4 spelling and grammar
-34
+ 5 vocabulary word
-29 Friendly Letter Format Test

(71)

Demetrius
September 30, 1988

807 S.E. 2nd Terr. -10
Gainesville, FL 32601
September 30, 1988

Dear Hairy Beast,
+5 Vocabulary
We are friends. You are a dulcet -1
-1 and thoughtful, and kind beast. Hilda
is greeting you wrong. She is a crummy sp. -1
girl. I don't like her. She is fat and
big. She has a long nose.

Sincerely Yours -10 -10
Demetrius

Demetrius — Good use of vocabulary
word! Be careful with the
letter format! You made
three careless errors. I
know you can do better!
See me and retake the test.
Mrs. K.

7th grade regular student.

The Dreaded Spelling

I am an English teacher who detests spelling. I am of the firm belief that a person is born either a good speller or a rotten speller, and nothing can be done about the latter except a gene change. I always have been a terrible speller myself, but I know how to use the dictionary or the speller on my computer very effectively. I have a dictionary in almost every room of my house and at several strategic locations in my classroom. When I was a little girl, however, I always earned a hundred on my spelling tests. I memorized the words and then promptly forgot them three minutes after the test. After sixteen years of teaching, I have found that my students are either like me or have a natural gift for spelling. Sometimes the poorest grammar students are the best spellers!

Most parents and school systems, however, still believe in spelling and insist that we teach it in our English classes. There are also certain basic words that must be learned even by the worst speller if he or she ever hopes to be an effective writer. I suggest two ways to teach spelling, both of which I have found to have more results than any other I have ever used. Both use an aspect of the Caught'ya. The first uses the story, and the second uses the vocabulary words.

SPELLING METHOD #1
(Appropriate for middle or elementary school)

Carol Harrell, a colleague of mine at Westwood Middle School, came up with a list of forty "Spelling Killers" that seem to be impossible for any middle schooler to spell or use correctly. Most of these words are homonyms. My friends who teach high school assure me that their students have yet to master these words too. I read memos and letters from adults, even teachers, who still misspell many of these forty words. You can probably guess what these words are before you see the list at the end of this chapter.

Carol's idea was to introduce only three or four words a week for thirteen weeks but to make them cumulative. If you introduce the dread "their, there, they're" the first week as Spelling List #1, then students are responsible for them on *every* spelling test for thirteen weeks. Tests, therefore, get longer and longer each week. The last test has forty words on it. By repeating and repeating these words, you increase the chances that your students will master them.

I have carried Carol's idea two steps further in my classroom. First, I put these words in the Caught'yas. If, for example, after a normal spelling lesson, the students still can't distinguish among "to, two, and too," I write these words into the Caught'yas until my students learn them.

I know that all the literature says that it is bad to spell a word wrong and to ask a child to correct it, but I feel that these homonyms are different. Because usage not spelling befuddles the students, I justify sometimes writing the incorrect homonym in the Caught'ya sentence. Sometimes I use the correct homonym; sometimes I do not. Whether or not I use the correct homonym, we *always* discuss which homonym should be used in the spot as well as why that homonym should be used.

My students are on the lookout for these words and never know whether I have used them correctly; therefore, they are forced to think each time. This thinking tends to result in mastery of correct usage of the homonyms. Notice in Chapters 6, 7, and 8 the repeated use of "their," "there," "they're" and "two," "to," "too" in the Caught'ya sentences.

Second, I took Carol's word list and made up practice spelling sentences to go along with whatever story I was using in my Caught'yas that year. Since these words are mostly homonyms, students need to practice them in the context of sentences, not in studying the letter order in the traditional way.

By using the Caught'ya plot, I can embellish the story and tell more detail than I can in the yearly 140 or so sentences of the Caught'yas. Carol's "Forty Spelling Killers" and thirteen of my practice spelling sheets appear at the end of this chapter.

Please note that I have included only the practice sheets for the middle school story of "Hairy Beast and Friends." These are suggested examples. You easily can write your own for any Caught'ya story you may be using. I use other spelling practice sheets the years I use other stories. They take only minutes to write. I usually don't even type them.

SPELLING METHOD #2
(Appropriate for advanced eighth grade and high school)

For this idea I modified a spelling system I heard about years ago. Nancie Atwell, however, suggests something similar in her book. (Atwell, 1987) This second method that I propose is an individualized spelling system. Don't groan! I have found that it really is possible without too many headaches. I now use this individualized method with my advanced eighth graders and have reduced the take-home work to about forty-five minutes per class once every two weeks!

The system is very simple. I begin the year by giving the Florida State Assessment Spelling List as a huge diagnostic test to provide my students with a base for spelling words. Other basic need-to-know spelling lists can be found in the back of most grammar books.

Every week each student must pick five (absolutely no more than five) words that he/she wants to learn to spell. After the students use the words that they misspelled on the diagnostic test, they choose words that they come across in the literature we read, vocabulary words from the Caught'yas that they want to use in their own writing (these are the most popular), and most importantly, words that they misspell in their writing.

My students take these five words and look them up in a dictionary. They list the dictionary page where they found the word, write the part of speech of the word, and rewrite the definition in their own words. They put two weeks' worth of spelling words on one piece of paper. They study these words.

Every two weeks they get together with their spelling partner, give each other a spelling test, and grade the tests together *very* carefully. I stress the word *"very"* since the spelling partner who earns the highest grade gets an extra five points added to that grade. This tends to keep them honest.

Students are responsible for these words all year. Every five weeks or so I give an oral spelling test. I ask my students for whatever spelling list I pick at random, collect them, and take a class period calling out two words to each child from his list. Since the students do not know which list I will use or which words I will call out, or even when I will give the test, they have to make sure that they always can spell all of the words on all of their lists all of the time. I give either a hundred or a fifty or a zero on these oral spelling tests.

Since students usually have only 140 spelling words a year that they picked themselves, neither they nor I feel that I am asking too much. Spelling words must be on the individual student's level. Some students use simpler words and others use more difficult ones. I keep track via writing efforts to determine which students are good spellers and which are not. Thus I can insist that my more competent spellers choose more sophisticated words. This avoids the tendency of teenagers to take the easy route.

Evaluating the written tests takes about forty-five minutes every two weeks. Since each child only has ten words, that helps a lot. The students hand in the word list along with the spelling test. I grade the tests with a dictionary on my lap. If I find a misspelled word that also is misspelled on the word list, the student loses twenty points instead of ten. This is because the word was not copied correctly from the dictionary. Such a practice encourages care on the part of students. Note that I also subtract five points from a student's score if an error was missed on the partner's paper. This, too, fosters zealous care.

The Terrible Parts of Speech

It is often useful and a nice change to use other formats for the Caught'yas. If, for example, you wish to review the parts of speech, you can instruct students to underline all adverbs or circle all conjunctions, etc. in the Caught'ya for the day. When I do this, I often write the Caught'ya correctly, and I usually include just one part of speech per Caught'ya. Since you have 180 days to play with and only eight parts of speech, you can take it slowly. While I know that it is unpopular to teach the parts of speech these days, I also recognize that learning the appropriate labels and usages for words is important. I also teach French, and students who are not familiar with the parts of speech in English are at a great disadvantage. You have to categorize words somehow. Learning the parts of speech makes sense.

In the Caught'ya example on the following page, students practice identifying adverbs. The example is followed by a student paper to show you how a child handles such an assignment. It is from the Hairy Beast story in Chapter 7. Please note that after students complete such a Caught'ya, you must initiate a discussion of the part of speech in question and perhaps give some oral drill in identifying that part of speech.

Once you have covered all the parts of speech, you can recite all eight of them daily for reinforcement purposes. It also helps to find a catchy mnemonic. *For example: "PAVPANIC — preposition, adverb, verb, pronoun, adjective, noun, interjection, conjunction."*

Example of Caught'ya Used to Teach
Parts of Speech

This goes on the blackboard:

Kind-hearted Bertha became very worried about Hairy. She went hurriedly to Hairy's apartment. There, she knocked timidly. It was ***intimidating***!

(*Underline the four adverbs.*)

This is a student's rendition:

Sabrina
October 16, 1989

Caught'ya

Monday
Kind-hearted Bertha became very (-1)
worried about Hairy. She went hurriedly
to Hairy's apartment. Adverb There she knocked
timidly.   It was intimidating !

7th grade regular student.

Sentence Diagramming

Diagramming sentences can be approached in much the same way. Put the Caught'ya on the board without any errors. Ask your students to diagram it. This assumes that you have previously instructed your students in the basics of how to diagram sentences. The first time I start out very simply with only subject and verb and then in subsequent Caught'yas" slowly add adjectives, adverbs, prepositional phrases, compound subjects and verbs, etc. as soon as my students feel comfortable. Since students are diagramming only one sentence a day, they do not find the assignment too cumbersome.

Again, many English teachers today frown on diagramming sentences. I find that taken in moderation and approached like a puzzle, sentence diagramming can be very helpful, especially to scientifically- and mathematically-minded students who need to see the entire picture before they can understand it. Diagramming sentences can be a tool to reach students who otherwise see no sense in learning proper English usage.

The practice of diagramming sentences has another advantage. It helps teach children how to think logically. They have to concentrate on the relationship among the words in order to diagram a sentence correctly.

Please note that you can ask your students to diagram only part of a Caught'ya by underlining that part and by simply telling them to diagram only that part. The following example that comes from the fourth story suggestion in Chapter 5 shows how to present such a Caught'ya to your students. After the example is a student paper that illustrates how children handle this assignment.

Example of Caught'ya Used to Teach Diagramming

This goes on the blackboard:

Then everyone quickly hid behind his locker.

Este screamed **raucously** when she saw the pictures.

(Diagram the underlined sentence and circle all adverbs and adverb phrases.)

Here's how one student handled this assignment:

7th grade regular student.

Writing Assignments and "Showing" Writing

You can take your story line as far as you want in student writing assignments. I usually like to elicit a description of the various characters in my Caught'ya story in a series of descriptive writing assignments. We practice writing letters to various characters. Halfway through the year I assign students to write possible twists and endings to the Caught'ya story. Students even write entire stories as offshoots of the basic Caught'ya plot. Such assignments sometimes are suggested by the students!

Rebekah Caplan, in her book *Showing Writing: A Training Program to Help Students Be Specific* introduces the concept of "Show Not Tell" writing assignments. (Caplan, 1980) These are short, seven-sentence paragraphs designed to force students to use the strong verbs so important to effective writing. Essentially, the teacher provides a topic sentence that contains a weak, inactive verb such as "am," "are," "is," "was," or "were." Students copy this sentence and add six more sentences of their own. Five of the six sentences use strong verbs. The last sentence is a conclusion. A weak, inactive verb is allowed in this last wrap-up sentence.

The example below, is a typical "Show Not Tell" paragraph. I copied it from a paper of a regular seventh grade student. The character described in the paragraph comes from the fourth Caught'ya story suggested in Chapter 5. Note the use of strong verbs, vocabulary word, and simile. The student absorbed the use of these sophisticated writing techniques through daily Caught'ya practice.

The Snob

May Bellina was a snob. Her nose stuck way up in the air like a ramp for rockets. She snubbed anyone who wasn't popular. Rings dripped from her polished fingers. She talked in only big words that no normal person could understand. Even her dog **cringed** under her glare. She was a genuine snob.

Since you are forcing your students to keep to a strict format, the paragraphs are contrived. Despite this artificiality, they can be very effective in making students aware of the power of using strong verbs. The funnier the topic you use, the more inventive your students' paragraphs will be. My personal favorite is to describe the school lunchroom and show that it was wild. Descriptions of Caught'ya characters fit well in these paragraphs.

Here are a few more samples copied from student papers. These examples were generated from the Caught'ya story in Chapter 7, "Hairy Beast and Friends." Some are letters. Some are "Show Not Tell" paragraphs.

Samples Faithfully Copied from Student Papers, Errors and All

None of these seventh grade students was advanced in language arts. In fact, some of them were rather weak in English skills. All of their grammar, mechanics, and usage that year was learned only from Caught'yas. I left in the students' errors, so you can see what they did (or did not) learn.

Joana's friendly letter:

> 3022 N. W. 24th Terr.
> Hogtown, FL 32606
> October 28, 1988

Dear Hairy Beast,

I'm really sad for you! What Hilda Hippo told you is not true. I love your green fur, your zits, and you are a very nice beast!

> Sincerely yours,
> Joana

Maggi's friendly letter:

817 N. W. 21st Terr.
Hogtown, FL 32603
October 28, 1988

Dear Hairy Beast,

I am sorry for your loss but rember *(sic)* she is not the only girl in the world. Hairy, there are other fish in the sea. Hey, maybe she's just sick, and if she's not, maybe I'll go out with you. Well, you'll be alright. *(sic)* Don't worry.

P.S. Here is my phone number just in case: 376 - 0751.

Your friend,
Maggi

Jennifer's description of Hairy Beast:

Hairy Beast

Hairy is ugly. His face sprouts warts that actually glow in the dark. They also grow as fast as grass. Hairy buys his clothes at the Salvation Army, garage sales, and his favorite of all stores, Flea World. He just adores pizza and Coke. Green beans are his favorite too. He also likes minted chocolate chip ice cream with snail fudge on it. His feet stink because he washes them in amonia. *(sic)* His feet shake the ground when he walks. Green fur streches *(sic)* out on both sides of his feet. He is a weird looking beast! Hairy helps people in a kind way. Hairy did love Hilda Hippo, but she dumped him. He would never hurt anyone's feelings. Hilda just couldn't see his inward appearances. Even though Hairy is ugly on the outside, he can be a really beautiful person on the inside.

Jason's description of Hilda Hippo:

(Please note use of vocabulary word.)

Hilda Hippo

While Hairy was ugly, Hilda was no prize herself. Her wide hips stuck out two feet from her fat body like football padding. Her size twelve feet stank worse than rotting garbage. Her **visage** scared little kids because of her mean expression. Hilda's hair hung down straight in strings. Her fat body blobbed up and down whenever she walked. I think Hairy is prettier, warts and all. Hilda is no prize.

Tests

Y ou can adapt the Caught'ya format for tests, too. Catherine Berg, now teaching at Gainesville High School, showed me how to automate these tests so we could grade them on the machine. Imagine an English test that can be scanned on a computerized test sheet!

At the end of this chapter, I have included four tests, two of which can be machine graded. The first test is for elementary students and is based on the "Magic Purple Umbrella" story told in Chapter 6. It can be used as a semester exam and can be machine graded. Use it again at the end of the year to test improvement.

The second and third tests are also for middle school students. They expand the story in Chapter 7 about Hairy Beast. One is an an end-of-the-year final exam designed for the computerized machine.

The fourth test is for high school students and is based on the revised tale of "Romeo and Juliet" found in Chapter 8. It, too, can be machine scored.

On the non-automated tests, students are instructed simply to write corrections on the ditto sheet. On the computerized tests, however, I instruct students to mark on the test itself the proofreading symbols they use in the daily Caught'yas *before* they attempt to put the answers on the computerized answer sheet. The only drawback to these automated tests is that you must have a machine that can handle more than one answer per number. Check to see if your school is equipped with such a machine.

Note that I have told my students how many paragraphs are in the test. This helps the weaker students. These tests are designed for average students. You can simplify them or make them more difficult according to the particular needs of your classes.

If you use a different story in your Caught'yas or want to test different skills, you can make up your own test. It is very easy to do. Simply take the Caught'ya story that you are using and add a few details to expand it into the test. In your test, make sure you include all the skills you have been stressing in the Caught'yas. You will be delighted with the results.

Hype

This is an extremely important aspect of the Caught'yas. The more you play up the good-natured teasing and encouragement while your students are working on the Caught'ya sentence, the better chance you have of "turning your students on" to language arts. Over the nine years that I have been using the Caught'yas in my classroom, the feedback from my students has been unanimous. Humor is an essential ingredient in your approach to the Caught'yas. Even after doing Caught'yas four days a week all year long, my students are as anxious to see if I "caught 'em" in May as they are in August.

As an English teacher you really are a public relations person for the English language. Let's be realistic. We have to compete with television, rock groups, and toughest of all, our students' peers. We have to inject fun into our teaching. I suggest bulletin boards with the characters of your Caught'ya story comically displayed. Try dressing up as one of your characters on Halloween or on the day of a Caught'ya test.

If you teach elementary school, you might want to make a "dress-up-as-your-favorite-Caught'ya-character" day. Middle school students really enjoy art work associated with the story. I often have a "design Hairy Beast contest." In high school, one has to be more subtle.

Any suggestions? Please write me via the publisher.

Whatever you do to advertise language arts, keep it light and humorous like the Caught'yas themselves. Most of all, have a good time yourself. Your enjoyment will be infectious.

Sample Spelling Practices

Key for Spelling Practices

Sample Caught'ya Tests

Keys

40 Spelling Killers

Week 1	Week 6	Week 10
there	threw	finally
their	through	probably
they're	thought	its
		it's
Week 2	Week 7	
know	believe	Week 11
no	friend	forty
	receive	ninety
Week 3	weird	
you're		Week 12
your	Week 8	a lot
	hole	although
Week 4	whole	Wednesday
were	write	
we're	right	Week 13
	rite	all together
Week 5		altogether
to	Week 9	all ready
too	quite	already
two	quit	
	quiet	

Weekly Spelling Schedule

Monday   Go over the new words with the class for parts of speech and meanings. Write a sentence with the class for each word. Students copy sentences, meanings, and parts of speech into their notebooks.

Thursday   Review words briefly in an oral drill. Students complete the practice sheet for homework.

Friday   Give spelling test after checking the practice sheet. Each test is on all words covered to that point. It's a good idea to dictate sentences for most of the tests. Students write the entire sentence. This is excellent for listening skills practice.

Every day   Reinforce spelling words by using them in the Caught'yas.

Week #1

Name _____

Date _____

Period _____

there   their   they're

1. _____ are many animals living in Hogtown.

2. _____ is a couple who is going together.

3. _____ names are Wilfred Warthog and Bertha Boa.

4. _____ always getting invited to parties!

5. The other animals of Hogtown, except for corpulent Hilda Hippo, enjoy _____ company.

6. Hilda Hippo constantly meddles in _____ affairs.

7. Hilda Hippo doesn't even care if she hurts_____ feelings.

8. Hilda decides to use Hairy Beast, _____ good friend.

9. _____ unaware that Hilda can be so cruel.

10. _____ very forgiving and believe that deep down _____ is goodness in Hilda Hippo.

Week #2

Name _____

Date _____

Period _____

know   no

1. Do you _____ a kind boa constrictor
   named Bertha?

2. Hilda Hippo never takes _____ for an
   answer.

3. Bertha Boa and Hairy Beast _____ that
   Wilfred Warthog is good-hearted.

4. Hairy Beast never says _____ to a good
   party.

5. _____, Hairy cannot date Hilda anymore.

6. After Hilda jilted him, Hairy Beast was sad and didn't
   _____ what to do.

7. Does Hilda _____ Hairy is so sad?

8. What will happen? Bertha Boa doesn't_____.

9. I don't _____ what Hairy is going to do.

10. Do you _____ what Hairy is going to
    do?

Week #3

Name _____

Date _____

Period _____

your   you're

1. _____ aware that Hairy Beast is in hysterics.

2. _____ certain Hairy cried for days and days.

3. In _____ opinion, is Hairy being ridiculous?

4. Is it _____ belief that Hairy has flipped his wig over Hilda Hippo?

5. I would like to think that _____ sympathetic towards Hairy.

6. _____ feelings on this subject might be mixed.

7. _____ probably having doubts about the characters in this soap opera.

8. Hairy Beast might actually remind you of one of _____ friends.

9. _____ friend might even resemble Hairy Beast!

10. Even though you may think this, _____ _____ best friend's best friend.

Week #4

Name _____

Date _____

Period _____

were   we're

1. _____ you aware that Hilda Hippo jilted Hairy Beast?

2. _____ certain that Hairy Beast has suffered tremendously.

3. Wilfred Warthog and Bertha Boa_____ sure that Hairy, their best friend, was depressed.

4. Wilfred and Bertha _____ trying to comfort Hairy.

5. Both _____ searching for Hairy in order to console him.

6. Hilda, _____ told, laughed when she sent Hairy that nasty letter.

7. _____ appalled that she could be so cruel.

8. _____ anxious for Hairy's friends to find him.

9. Wilfred and Bertha _____ certain that Hairy would recover.

10. _____ Hilda and Hairy ever really a match made in heaven?

Week #5

Name _____

Date _____

Period _____

to   too   two

1. Bertha Boa decided _____ comfort Hairy Beast by sending him flowers.

2. Wilfred Warthog tried _____ comfort him _____.

3. Unfortunately, Wilfred's letter was _____ pompous.

4. Hairy's tears flowed for _____ hours when he received Wilfred's letter.

5. Hairy had been hurt _____ many times.

6. He just couldn't face his _____ closest friends anymore.

7. Hairy finally began _____ realize that Hilda had never really loved him, that she was _____ cold-hearted.

8. He saw that Hilda Hippo was_____ wrapped up in herself.

9. It took _____ weeks of hiding in his bathtub before Hairy Beast finally realized this.

10. Wilfred and Bertha didn't feel that they had gotten _____ involved with their friend. They loved him _____ much.

Week #6

Name _____

Date _____

Period _____

threw   through   thought

1. Hairy Beast _____ Wilfred Warthog was a good friend.

2. When Hairy received Wilfred's letter, he wanted to throw it _____ the window.

3. Instead, he shredded it and _____ it into the garbage where he _____ it belonged.

4. He also _____ out the remains of Bertha's flowers after he had eaten most of them.

5. He was _____ with making any more friends of any kind, and he _____ he could survive life on his own, so he went to bed.

6. Hairy dreamed that he went to work and walked _____ the halls of General Animal Hospital.

7. He was in deep _____ when the lights suddenly went out.

8. Hairy tripped over a chair and fell _____ a doorway into the arms of Hilda Hippo.

9. Hairy then _____ he was dreaming.

10. He was right. He woke up and _____ the covers off his bed when he _____ he heard the alarm clock ring.

Week #7

Name _____

Date _____

Period _____

believe   friend   receive   weird

1. Hairy was a _____ beastie with green fur.

2. Hairy didn't _____ that Hilda was using him.

3. When he _____d and read Hilda's letter, he was devastated.

4. Hairy's _____ behavior was almost uncontrollable, and his _____s didn't think that he would recover any time soon.

5. Bertha Boa considered Hairy Beast to be a dear _____ .

6. Bertha wrote Wilfred a letter to ask what was wrong with their _____ Hairy Beast.

7. We know that Hairy Beast also _____d a pompous note from Wilfred.

8. We _____ that Wilfred unintentionally sent that letter, that he did not_____ that it was pompous when he wrote it.

9. We hope that Wilfred will apologize to his _____ Hairy.

10. _____ Hairy will hopefully recover from the mishap and be Wilfred's _____ again.

Week #8

Name _____

Date _____

Period _____

whole   hole   write   right   rite

1. We know that Hilda performed the cruel_____ of sending Hairy a "Dear John" letter to give him the brush-off.

2. Hilda intentionally wanted to _____ such a nasty, scathing letter to poor Hairy.

3. The _____ letter was full of hatred and spite.

4. We are _____ to dislike Hilda as Hairy was _____ to hide in his hiding _____until he felt better.

5. Hairy was _____ to cry so many tears, and he was unable to _____ a letter back to Hilda in reply.

6. Hairy must have felt like digging a_____ and crawling _____ inside it when he received that cruel letter.

7. Hairy experienced the _____ of unrequited love.

8. The _____ incident was unfortunate.

9. Wilfred wanted to _____ a note to console his friend Hairy.

10. Bertha sent Hairy a _____, big bouquet of flowers following the American_____ of sending flowers to sad loved ones.

Week #9

Name _____

Date _____

Period _____

quite   quit   quiet

1. When Hairy received that awful letter from Hilda, he couldn't _____ crying for two weeks.

2. The letter was _____ upsetting.

3. Hairy couldn't _____ his loud sobbing; he just couldn't be _____ with his tears.

4. We know he'll have _____ a time recovering from the break-up with Hilda because he can't _____ loving her.

5. Hairy retreated into hiding for some peace and _____ .

6. This whole incident was _____ a tale of woe.

7. We hope that Hairy won't _____ going to parties.

8. Bertha and Wilfred think that Hilda is _____ a snob.

9. We hope that Hilda will _____ torturing poor Hairy and that he will finally _____ loving her.

10. We hope that Bertha and Wilfred won't _____ trying to comfort Hairy in his time of need.

Week #10   Name _____

                                      Date _____

                                      Period _____

finally   probably   its   it's

1. Hilda's letter to Hairy was appalling, and_____
   contents were downright cruel.

2. After Hairy trashed his apartment, _____
   decor was a mess.

3. _____ unfortunate Hairy has been so shaken up
   that he won't be able to clean his apartment for a while.

4. _____ quite upsetting to be jilted by a girl friend.

5. The break-up devastated Hairy, but perhaps he will
   realize that _____ _____ for the best.

6. Hairy will _____ welcome some
   reassurance from his closest friends at their party.

7. Wilfred _____ realized that his letter to
   Hairy was pompous and went to see his friend.

8. After Wilfred hugged Hairy and apologized for his
   pompous letter, he _____ listened to
   Hairy's tale of woe and all _____ grisly
   facts.

9. Hairy will _____ recover if he can face
   Hilda and realize what a nasty lady she really is.

10. _____ , Hairy's warts will _____ go
    away as he recovers.

Week #11

Name _____

Date _____

Period _____

forty   ninety

1. Hairy will be with about _____ of his friends at Wilfred's and Bertha's party.

2. He probably felt _____ years old after Hilda rejected him.

3. Hairy could have cried and moaned for_____ days and _____ nights.

4. Hairy's friends were worried that he might not recover for more than _____ or even _____ days.

5. They therefore threw a party and invited more than _____ of Hairy's friends and neighbors.

6. At the party Wilfred and Hairy talked for over _____ minutes and didn't realize that almost an hour had gone by.

7. Meanwhile, Bertha made _____ sausage rolls in the kitchen because she didn't have enough dough to make an even hundred.

8. Fat Hilda Hippo weighs much more than one hundred and _____ pounds!

9. Her hips stick out at least _____ inches.

10. She looks as if she is middle-aged and at least_____ years old.

Name _____

Date _____

Period _____

a lot   although   Wednesday

1. There are _____ of unusual characters in Hogtown.

2. _____ Hairy did _____ of crying and moaning after Hilda rejected him, he may finally recover.

3. _____ Wilfred and Bertha wanted to have their party on a _____, they could only have it on a Saturday.

4. They invited _____ of Hairy's friends and neighbors who all said that they couldn't come on a _____ .

5. It took _____ of guts for Hairy to come to the party and for him to stick his tongue out at Hilda.

6. Hairy and Wilfred went to Hilda's house to insult her on a _____ because Hairy felt that it was his good-luck day.

7. _____ all of Hairy's friends tried to console him at the party, it may still take _____ of time for him to completely recover.

8. _____ Hairy has suffered through _____, he will eventually recover.

9. He has _____ of hidden strength.

10. Maybe by next _____ he will feel better and be _____ like his former, happy self.

Week #13　　　　　　　Name _____

　　　　　　　　　　　　Date _____

　　　　　　　　　　　　Period _____

　　　　all together　　altogether　　all ready　　already

1. Bertha asked, "Is everyone _____ to go shopping?"

2. They planned to go to the store _____ in one car.

3. "I _____ went shopping before I went into hiding," murmured poor Hairy.

4. Bertha impatiently asked again, "Is everyone _____ to go? I'm _____ getting anxious about Saturday's party."

5. "I would _____ rather we see a movie," sighed Wilfred who hated to go shopping even _____ with his friends.

6. "I'm _____ walking to the car," said Bertha in exasperation as she stepped out the door of the apartment.

7. Once at the store Wilfred insisted that they walk _____ in a straight line with Hairy in the middle.

8. When they all couldn't make up their minds about what to buy, Bertha accused them of being _____ too indecisive.

9. Bertha swore that she would never go shopping _____ with her friends.

10. She was _____ disgusted with her friends and was _____ to send them all home and do the shopping herself.

Key for Spelling Practice Sheets

Week 1
1. There
2. There
3. Their
4. They're
5. their
6. their
7. their
8. their
9. They're
10. They're, there

Week 2
1. know
2. no
3. know
4. no
5. No
6. know
7. know
8. know
9. know
10. know

Week 3
1. You're
2. You're
3. your
4. your
5. you're
6. Your
7. You're
8. your
9. Your
10. you're, your

Week 4
1. Were
2. We're
3. were
4. were
5. were
6. we're
7. We're
8. We're
9. were
10. Were

Week 5
1. to
2. to, too
3. too
4. two
5. too
6. two
7. to, too
8. too
9. two
10. too, too

Week 6
1. thought
2. through
3. threw, thought
4. threw
5. through, thought
6. through
7. thought
8. through
9. thought
10. threw, thought

Week 7
1. weird
2. believe
3. received
4. weird, friends
5. friend
6. friend
7. received
8. believe, believe
9. friend
10. Weird, friend

Week 8
1. rite
2. write
3. whole
4. right, right, hole
5. right, write
6. hole, right
7. rite
8. whole
9. write
10. whole, rite

Week 9
1. quit
2. quite
3. quit, quiet
4. quite, quit
5. quiet
6. quite
7. quit
8. quite
9. quit, quit
10. quit

Week 10
1. its
2. its
3. It's
4. It's
5. it's, probably
6. probably
7. finally
8. finally, its
9. probably
10. Finally, probably

Week 11
1. forty or ninety
2. ninety
3. forty, forty or ninety, ninety
4. forty, ninety
5. forty or ninety
6. forty
7. ninety
8. ninety or forty
9. forty or ninety
10. forty

Week 12
1. a lot
2. Although, a lot
3. Although, Wednesday
4. a lot, Wednesday
5. a lot
6. Wednesday
7. Although, a lot
8. Although, a lot
9. a lot
10. Wednesday, a lot

Week 13
1. all ready
2. all together
3. already
4. all ready, already
5. altogether, all together
6. already
7. all together
8. altogether
9. all together
10. altogether, all ready

Four Sample Caught'ya Tests

Caught'ya TEST -　　　　Name _____
Elementary School　　　　Date _____

Directions:　　Write in the corrections on this paper. Work carefully and check your work. This is just one big Caught'ya.

marys magic purple umbrella

mary will never forget the day the old lady came to her classroom. that was the day she got her magic purple umbrella. mary and her class planned to travel all over the world with their umbrellas. they hoped to visit italy england russia france and china.

one day marys grandmother became sick. marys grandmother however lived far away from mary in hope montana. mary wanted to cheer up her grandmother and she wanted to see if her grandmother was all right. mary went to her teacher. i want to use my umbrella to visit my grandmother she said.

thats not possible said the teacher.

why not asked mary.

you have to travel with an adult answered marys teacher.

mary and her nice kind teacher talked for a while. marys teacher agreed to go visit marys grandmother after school that day but they needed to take another child along to fly the teacher. mary found her best friend susie thompson. mary went home to get a picture of her grandmother.

that afternoon the 3 held hands put up their umbrellas and stared at the picture of marys grandmother. in less than 1 minute they were at marys grandmothers house. marys grandmother was delighted to see mary and she told mary that she felt better already. oh boy mary was relieved.

Caught'ya TEST -
Elementary School

Name __Key__

Date _____

Directions: Write in the corrections on this paper. Work carefully and work. This is just one big Caught'ya.

Mary's Magic Purple Umbrella

Mary will never forget the day the old lady came to her classroom. That was the day she got her magic purple umbrella. Mary and her class planned to travel all over the world with their umbrellas. They hoped to visit Italy, England, Russia, France, and China.

One day Mary's grandmother became sick. Mary's grandmother, however, lived far away from Mary in Hope, Montana. Mary wanted to cheer up her grandmother, and she wanted to see if her grandmother was all right. Mary went to her teacher. "I want to use my umbrella to visit my grandmother," she said.

"That's not possible," said the teacher.

"Why not?" asked Mary.

"You have to travel with an adult," answered Mary's teacher.

Mary and her nice, kind teacher talked for a while. Mary's teacher agreed to go visit Mary's grandmother after school that day, but they needed to take another child along to fly the teacher. Mary found her best friend, Susie Thompson. Mary went home to get a picture of her grandmother.

That afternoon the three held hands, put up their umbrellas, and stared at the picture of Mary's grandmother. In less than one minute they were at Mary's grandmother's house. Mary's grandmother was delighted to see Mary, and she told Mary that she felt better already. Oh boy, Mary was relieved.

Caught'ya TEST -   Name _____

Middle School Semester Test   Date _____

Directions: Write in the corrections on this paper. Work carefully and check your work. This is just one big Caught'ya. There are three paragraphs. I have indented the first and the third paragraphs. Mark the second one with the paragraph symbol.

the latest gossip from general animal hospital

their is alot of news from hogtown florida. warty repulsive hairy beast is no longer ugly nor is he despondent. hairy has had a face lift and has found a lovely new girlfriend. the face lift was a total success and hairy is almost handsome. hairy is delighted. hairys new girlfriend is gorgeous vivacious and kind-hearted amanda armadillo. amanda used to go with boris warthog a long time ago but boris left amanda when he fell in love with bertha. lucky handsome hairy adores his new girl and she loves hairy. hairy hopes that their will be alot of parties to attend so that he can show her off. as she looks at her new handsome boyfriend amanda feels lucky.

hello friends say amanda and hairy.

Caught'ya TEST -
Middle School Semester Test

Name _____

Date _____

Directions: Write in the corrections on this paper. Work carefully and check your work. This is just one big Caught'ya. There are three paragraphs. I have indented the first and the third paragraphs. Mark the second one with the paragraph symbol.

The Latest Gossip from General Animal Hospital

There is a lot of news from Hogtown, Florida. Warty, repulsive Hairy Beast is no longer ugly nor is he despondent. Hairy has had a face lift and has found a lovely, new girlfriend. The face lift was a total success, and Hairy is almost handsome. Hairy is delighted. ¶ Hairys' new girlfriend is gorgeous, vivacious, and kind-hearted Amanda Armadillo. Amanda used to go with Boris Warthog a long time ago, but Boris left Amanda when he fell in love with Bertha. Lucky, handsome Hairy adores his new girl, and she loves Hairy. Hairy hopes that there will be a lot of parties to attend so that he can show her off. As she looks at her new handsome boyfriend, Amanda feels lucky.

"Hello, friends," say Amanda and Hairy.

Caught'ya TEST -   Name_____

Middle School End-of-Year Test   Date _____

(May be machine scored.)

Directions: *First* correct the big Caught'ya. *Next*,
              on the answer sheet, mark the letter
              of the correction(s) needed for each
              number.

HINT!!! There are 7 paragraphs.
Remember to begin a new paragraph
whenever a different person speaks.

A - Begin paragraph before this word.
B - Put quotation marks before or after
    this word.
C - Put a comma after this word.
D - Capitalize.
E - Put an apostrophe in this word.

                general animal hospital revisited
                  1   2   3   4
hilda hairys vituperative ex-girlfriend abruptly boarded a
      5   6   7
plane flew away and headed for thrilling new adventures in
  8   9
tibet. hogtown florida will not be the same without her
  10   11   12   13
cried her viewers. good riddance! shes going to make
              14   15
trouble wherever she goes sneered resentful hairy beast.   no
                      16   17   18   19
i dont think so replied bertha because shes learned her
20 21   22   23   24   25
lesson. boris warthog added well i still think shes a
  26   27   28   29   30 31   32
troublemaker but maybe shell find happiness in tibet. i
    33   34   35   36
hope so boris replied kind bertha. we could sure use some
  37 38   39   40
peace and quiet around here! arrogant arthur aardvark
                        41   42   43   44
newest resident of hogtown florida snickered slyly to
                     45   46
himself fools! the fun is just beginning in this hick town!
  47   48   49   50

Caught'ya TEST -
Middle School End-of-Year Test

Name **Key**

Date _____

(May be machine scored.)

Directions: *First* correct the big Caught'ya. *Next,* on the answer sheet, mark the letter of the correction(s) needed for each number.

HINT!!! There are 7 paragraphs. Remember to begin a new paragraph whenever a different person speaks.

A - Begin paragraph before this word.
B - Put quotation marks before or after this word.
C - Put a comma after this word.
D - Capitalize.
E - Put an apostrophe in this word.

1.	D
2.	D
3.	D
4.	D
5.	ACD
6.	DE
7.	C
8.	C
9.	C
10.	D
11.	ABCD
12.	DC
13.	BC
14.	ABD
15.	DE
16.	BC
17.	D
18.	D
19.	ABCD
20.	D
21.	E
22.	BC
23.	CD
24.	B
25.	E
26.	B
27.	AD
28.	D
29.	C
30.	BCD
31.	D
32.	E
33.	C
34.	E
35.	BD
36.	ABD
37.	C
38.	BCD
39.	D
40.	BD
41.	B
42.	AD
43.	D
44.	CD
45.	CD
46.	CD
47.	C
48.	BD
49.	D
50.	B

General Animal Hospital Revisited

Hilda Hairys vituperative ex-girlfriend, abruptly boarded a plane, flew away, and headed for thrilling new adventures in Tibet. "Hogtown, Florida, will not be the same without her, cried her viewers. "Good riddance! Shes going to make trouble wherever she goes, sneered resentful Hairy Beast. "No, I dont think so, replied Bertha, "because shes learned her lesson." Boris Warthog added, "Well, I still think shes a troublemaker, but maybe shell find happiness in Tibet." "I hope so, Boris, replied kind Bertha. "We could sure use some peace and quiet around here!" Arrogant Arthur Aardvark, newest resident of Hogtown, Florida, snickered slyly to himself, "Fools! The fun is just beginning in this hick town!"

Caught'ya TEST -
High School End-of-Year Test
(May be machine scored.)

Name_____
Date _____

Directions: *First* correct the big Caught'ya.
Next, on the answer sheet, mark the letter of
the correction(s) needed for each number.

HINT!!!   There are 10 paragraphs.

A - Begin paragraph before this word.
B - Put quotation marks before or after this word.
C - Put a comma after this word.
D - Capitalize.
E - Put an apostrophe in this word.

the sequel to romeo and juliet
oh romeo sighed juliet isnt it nice that we are allowed to
go together? yes youre right agreed her beau. lets get out
of this creepy mausoleum and boogie cried juliet as she
bolted for the open door of the crypt. yes lets get out of
here echoed romeo. as the year wore on romeo began to
get ticked with juliets flighty ways. she always wanted to
party and she always wanted to be on the go. romeo a
much quieter person preferred to have library dates. juliet
began to complain to her friends. well cressida and
miranda hes getting awfully boring she wailed. i didn't
realize that he was such a four-eyed dip. all he wants to
do is read or study she continued. how awful and boring
cried juliets friends. hes so cute but he sounds so dull.
he is dull retorted juliet. then dump him suggested her
helpful friends. i will decided juliet. They broke up the
next day.

Caught'ya TEST -
High School End-of-Year Test
(May be machine scored.)

Name_____Key_____
Date_____

Directions: *First* correct the big Caught'ya.
Next, on the answer sheet, mark the letter of the correction(s) needed for each number.

HINT!!! There are 10 paragraphs.

A - Begin paragraph before this word.
B - Put quotation marks before or after this word.
C - Put a comma after this word.
D - Capitalize.
E - Put an apostrophe in this word.

The Sequel to Romeo and Juliet

"Oh, Romeo," sighed Juliet, isn't it nice that we are allowed to go together?" "Yes, you're right," agreed her beau. "Lets get out of this creepy mausoleum and boogie," cried Juliet as she bolted for the open door of the crypt. "Yes, lets get out of here," echoed Romeo. As the year wore on, Romeo began to get ticked with Juliets flighty ways. She always wanted to party, and she always wanted to be on the go. Romeo, a much quieter person, preferred to have library dates. Juliet began to complain to her friends. "Well, Cressida and Miranda, hes getting awfully boring," she wailed. "I didn't realize that he was such a four-eyed dip. All he wants to do is read or study," she continued. "How awful and boring," cried Juliets friends. "Hes so cute, but he sounds so dull. If he is dull," retorted Juliet. "Then dump him," suggested her helpful friends. "I will," decided Juliet. They broke up the next day.

1. D
2. D
3. D
4. D
5. ABCD
6. BCD
7. CD
8. BE
9. B
10. ABCD
11. E
12. BC
13. ABDE
14. BC
15. D
16. ABCD
17. E
18. BC
19. D
20. AD
21. C
22. D
23. DE
24. D
25. C
26. CD
27. C
28. AD
29. BCD
30. D
31. CD
32. E
33. BC
34. BD
35. D
36. BC
37. ABD
38. BC
39. DE
40. BDE
41. C
42. B
43. ABD
44. BC
45. D
46. ABD
47. BC
48. ABD
49. BC
50. D

CHAPTER 5

Six Sample Story Ideas

Introduction to Story Suggestions

This chapter supplies six story ideas that you can modify, twist, and otherwise change to suit your needs. Only the bare bones of the plots are given. Using these plots, adjusted to your students' likes and dislikes, you can come up with your own daily Caught'ya sentence. Have fun!

I have suggested two plots for the elementary level, and two each for the middle school and high school levels. All the plot ideas, except that of "The Weird Class," have been road tested in various classrooms at the appropriate grade levels. I encountered only two problems: most of my advanced eighth graders who tested the "Romeo and Juliet Revised and Revisited" story insisted that Juliet was "a real dip," and one group of my seventh graders hated Hilda with such a passion that they booed whenever she entered the story.

Chapters 6, 7, and 8 of this book go one step further and have provided you with one hundred Caught'yas for one of the two story suggestions for each grade level. If at first you find it difficult to come up with your own sentences, you can use these. Take over with your own sentences whenever you feel comfortable.

Most of these plots are a community effort. Catherine Berg and I wrote the story of "General Animal Hospital." Carol Harrell, Laurel Harb, and I enjoyed coming up with "Hogtown Mean School," but it was Carol who provided the original idea for that story. I wrote the others myself but never would have thought of the "Romeo and Juliet Revised and Revisited" idea if it hadn't been for Jeannette Zesch who teaches in the Florida Adventist school system. Jeannette came to me to ask me to rewrite Shakespeare's story into daily Caught'yas. The end result of that request can be found in Chapter 8 of this book.

Other teachers in my county have written their own plots, all of which are amusing and imaginative. I have given talks about the Caught'ya for the Florida Council Teachers of English and the Florida Adventist School system and frequently get letters from teachers who attended those talks and who came up with their own successful story ideas. I also receive numerous requests for copies of what are Chapters 6, 7, and 8 of this book, so please, don't feel inadequate if you don't initially come up with your own story line or your own Caught'ya sentences.

I suggest that you first try to invent your own plot. If you find that chore too onerous this year, use one of my six suggestions. They are generic and should appeal to most children. If you then feel uncomfortable writing your own sentences, use Chapters 6, 7, or 8 until you want to branch out on your own. Send the publisher your best Caught'ya plots. They could be included in the planned sequel of this book, *Caught'ya Again!*, that will feature more Caught'yas.

Story Suggestions

Elementary School:

1. "The Magic Purple Umbrella"

This is a soap opera for the elementary crowd, third through fifth grades. Only the name of the school is changed. Imaginary students who have the same names and personalities as your students receive imaginary purple umbrellas with yellow polka dots. The old lady who presents these umbrellas to the students does so because the class is so very good. She tells them that the umbrellas can go anywhere the students wish, but there are three stipulations. First, no student can go anywhere without his teacher (and the umbrellas do not work for adults — kids love this). Second, no one can mention the umbrellas outside the classroom. Third, students have to continue to be well-behaved.

The clever students quickly discover how to transport their teacher (cooperation of several students), and the class treks all around the world. For extra drama, I also throw in two boys who try to take their umbrellas home and are punished by having non-working umbrellas for the next few days. At the end of the year, the old lady collects the umbrellas and tells the class how wonderful they have been. During the course of the year, add details such as the teacher's fear of heights and the subsequent results thereof.

The first year I used this story in a fifth grade classroom, one of my male students arrived in class one day with a purple polka-dotted umbrella smuggled in under his jacket. Where he had found it, I still don't know. I suspect he asked for it and received it for his birthday! The one hundred Caught'ya sentences of this plot can be found in Chapter 6.

2. "The Weird Class"

This is another soap opera for the elementary crowd. Change the name of the school but make the teachers and students magically have the same names as the teachers and students in your school. The students do all kinds of stunts to annoy the teacher and each other. (Use your students' favorite tricks.)

One day the teacher becomes ill. The class drives off two timid substitutes with their antics. Then the "horrible lady" appears and takes over the class. She is incredibly mean, with eyes in the back of her head. No one can get away with anything. She learns all the students' names in one day, and she makes them work harder than ever before. She looks bizarre (let your imagination run wild to describe her), and she definitely has no sense of humor.

The end result is that the students send flowers, get-well cards, and pictures to speed their regular teacher's recovery. Encouraged by her students' attention, the teacher becomes well and returns to school. The class is now reformed and appreciates her.

This story should be fun because students love to read about tricks that children play on adults especially when their names are the same as those of the protagonists (or should I say *antagonists*).

<u>Middle School:</u>

1. "General Animal Hospital"

This soap opera is my favorite. I also give you one hundred Caught'ya sentences of this story in Chapter 7. The soap can take place in Hogtown, Florida, or a thinly disguised version of your town. Various animals with silly names like Hairy Beast, Eggbert Elephant, Wilfred Warthog, and Hilda Hippo play, love, mourn, and carry on in true soap opera fashion.

Hairy Beast is supremely ugly (warts and all). It is a good idea to challenge your students to come up with a good description of this creature. Hairy may be grotesque, but he is kind and sensitive. He is madly in love with Hilda Hippo, a beautiful hippo with a hard heart. She writes Hairy a "Dear John" letter insulting Hairy's looks. Hairy is devastated.

Hairy Beast does all kinds of things in his anguish and finally holes up in his closet. His friends, Wilfred Warthog and Bertha Boa, try all kinds of antics to cheer him up, including taking Hairy to Hilda's house to stick his tongue out at her and show her his warts. Nothing seems to work, not even letters and flowers. At this point you can practice letter writing format by having Hairy's friends write him consoling notes in the daily Caught'yas

You can parallel this flurry of letter writing in the Caught'yas with a letter writing unit in which one of the assignments is to write to poor Hairy. In Chapter 4 of this book, you can read a few of the hilarious letters my students have produced.

Finally, Hairy's friends throw a huge party so everyone can meet the new dude in town, Eggbert Elephant. Eggbert is arrogant and pompous. At the party (middle schoolers love parties) everyone throws popcorn and has a great time. Hairy, persuaded by his friends, finally comes to the party.

There he sees Hilda flirt with Eggbert. He gets over her instantly. Hilda falls for Eggbert. After the party Hilda is jilted by Eggbert, and Hairy is vindicated. Hilda flies off to Tibet to look for a way to improve herself. Hairy and his friends continue their lives without her.

2. *"Name of your town* Mean School"

This is a soap opera about your school, thinly disguised. Make up names for the teachers and administrators in your school that make fun of the names and the personalities. For example, I am clumsy, and my name is Kiester, so I was renamed Mrs. Klutzer. Another teacher is sweet, but insistent about getting work handed in. Her name is Harrell, so she became Mrs. Hassle.

For the students in the story, invent various exaggerated characters (according to stereotypes in vogue that year) like Gerald the Nerd, Surfer Sam, and Surfette Sarah.

Keep the story simple. A couple of "cool" characters (surfers or whatever) find themselves transferred to your school. Your school happens to be full of nerds. The teachers are awful (play up all your nasty traits) and embarrassingly resemble the teachers in your school. These teachers torture the students with work about which the students complain.

Using some of the names of your students to liven up the interest, have the two "cool dudes" (who really are snobs) enter the school with horror. Spend a few months of Caught'yas describing the school and its inhabitants. Then have the "cool dudes" slowly realize that the "nerds" are really O.K. after all.

At first the "cool dudes" boycott the parties (describe these in great detail) and the dances. They try to fight (again great detail is always appreciated by students) the "nerds." The "cool" ones finally succumb to the niceness of the "nerds," enjoy themselves, and change into "nerds" themselves.

The climax of the story concerns the "cool dude" who falls madly in love with one of the "nerds." This "nerdette" even wears glasses! Of course she is wonderful underneath the "uncool" exterior and everyone ends up happily ever after. End the school year with a couple more "cool dudes" planning to transfer.

High School:

1. *"Name of your local mall slightly changed* Mall Revisited"

In this soap opera, all the main characters like Plain Jane, Lovely Linda and Handsome Harry, love, shop, and have jealous fantasies at a large shopping mall. They discuss everyone in your school and suffer typical teenage traumas. Again, you can use the names of some of your own students to liven up the interest. Parents can be the villains in this story by withholding money, dragging teens home, and so on. It's always good to throw in a rescue of some sort by an unpopular student who wears glasses. In this fashion, this student becomes popular.

In order to use this soap opera successfully, it is advisable to have student input on the escapades of the student characters. That way you find out what's on their agenda, and they feel as if they have a hand in their assignments.

Have a love triangle with the most handsome and popular boy in the school, the most gorgeous girl, and Plain Jane. Plain Jane wins the prize because of her niceness.

You can spend at least a month of Caught'yas describing the purchasing of clothes. Another month can be spent with the love triangle. If you have a drug problem in your school, have a few students get caught with dope at the mall. Again, I advise you to consult your students on this story line. They have fertile minds for scandalous ideas.

2. *"Romeo and Juliet* Revised"

Actually any literature that your students are reading will do for this story line, but I used *Romeo and Juliet* because it is read by all ninth graders in my county. Take the piece of literature and change it to fit your students' interests. Make sure there is a happy ending.

In *"Romeo and Juliet* Revised,"* the action takes place at the Verona Mall. There, Juliet and her friends, with names taken from other female characters of Shakespeare, buy clothes, complain about the stinginess of their clothing allowances, and envy the rich Cressida.

At a concert in the center of the mall, Juliet encounters Romeo. They fall instantly in love. The problem is that Juliet's family is snobbish, and Romeo's family is bohemian. The love affair is not approved by their respective parents. In fact, Juliet's parents keep trying to set her up with Paris, a rich young man from a prominent family. Juliet loathes Paris. Romeo and Juliet sneak to the mall to see each other. One day Juliet's cousin and Romeo's friends get into a fight in the parking lot of the mall. They fight over a fender-bender. The fight puts Tybalt and Mercutio in the hospital.

Romeo's parents arrive at the scene to drag off their son. Romeo is placed on restriction and banished to his grandmother's house fifty miles away. Juliet's parents also arrive on the scene and forbid Juliet ever to see Romeo again. Juliet's parents continue to push Paris at her. She secretly meets Romeo at the church (aided by Juliet's Aunt Nurse), and they decide to get married. The friendly pastor, the Reverend Laurence, talks them out of marriage since Juliet is only fourteen. Instead, the two teenagers decide to go steady.

They spend an innocent night talking in Juliet's room. Romeo leaves to hitchhike back to his grandmother's house, and Juliet is devastated. Pressured again by her parents to date Paris, Juliet runs away. She hides in her family's tomb, but forgets to bring food. She sends a note to Romeo, but it goes astray.

The Reverend Laurence finally writes a note to Romeo explaining the situation. Meanwhile, Juliet is starving in the tomb. She passes out. Romeo has to walk the fifty miles back to Verona. He enters the tomb and finds Juliet passed out. He is so exhausted from the walk that he goes to sleep. Juliet wakes up, eats the candy bar that Romeo always keeps in his pocket, and goes back to sleep beside Romeo.

The good Reverend decides that enough is enough and calls the parents of the two teenagers. Both sets of parents arrive at the tomb. Seeing their children asleep, they think that they are dead. The wise Reverend informs the distraught parents that all is well, but that they had better get their act together.

The parents decide that maybe it is all right for their children to go steady after all. Romeo and Juliet wake up to a happy reunion with the Reverend Laurence claiming that all's well that ends well.

I have borrowed flagrantly from Shakespeare for this story line. You can have discussions of the real story by asking your students just how the Caught'ya plot differs from the one by Shakespeare. In Chapter 8, I have included one hundred Caught'ya sentences of this story.

100 Sample Caught'yas

"The Magic Purple Umbrella"

Grades 3 - 5

Important Notes

In almost every Caught'ya, students will be required to separate fragments from sentences, capitalize the first letter of the sentence, and supply end punctuation. These are not, therefore, listed each time in the skills. Note, too, that there are blanks. Use these to fill in names and information about your class. Younger children love to have personalized Caught'yas where they are the protagonists.

There are only one hundred Caught'yas given here. If you do three a week, these one hundred sentences are all that you will need. If you do one Caught'ya a day, you'll need eighty more of them. Having to come up with some of your own gives you the flexibility to add sentences anywhere you wish. You can give more detail to the basic story line for more practice in the skills you determine are necessary. Older students, for example, will need more practice in punctuating quotes. You can make up a number of Caught'yas that include conversations. Younger students may need more practice with the comma rules. In fact, younger children may need more overall repetition of skills in order for mastery to take place.

In addition, for the younger grades you may wish to simplify the Caught'yas or leave in only a few of the errors. For the fifth grade you may wish to make the sentences longer. You can have your students travel all over the world with their umbrellas. Adapt the Caught'yas to suit your needs.

The vocabulary words are intended for fun, extra credit, and enrichment. They are not bound to one grade level. You will notice that some of the same vocabulary words are repeated for the elementary, middle, *and* high school levels. A fourth grader can have just as much fun with a ten-dollar word as a seventh grader or an eleventh grader. The only difference is that older students can use the word in their writing as well as in their speech.

The skills included in the one hundred sentences were not taken out of the air. I included the skills from state-adopted grammar books and from the curriculum guide for my county. The skills, however, are threaded through the sentences rather than presented in the usual textbook sequence.

Finally, let me emphasize that the Caught'ya method works. Use these sentences to forge a partnership with your students, a partnership that will result in improved writing, increased vocabulary, and lots of shared laughs.

Vocabulary Word and Skills	Daily Caught'ya (B-for board, C-for correct)
1. stupendous Paragraph Write out ordinal numbers Comma (city, state)	B - once upon a time there was a **stupendous** _____ grade class in _____ _____ C - Once upon a time there was a **stupendous** _____ grade class in _____ , _____ .
2. fantastic Abbreviation (Ms. Mr.)	B - this **fantastic** class just happened to have _____ as its teacher C - This **fantastic** class just happened to have _____ as its teacher.
3. pupils Homophone (there) Write out numbers of one and two words.	B - their were _____ **pupils** in this class C - There were _____ **pupils** in this class.
4. bizarre Paragraph Comma (2 adjectives)	B - one fine sunny day something **bizarre** happened to this stupendous class C - One fine, sunny day something **bizarre** happened to this stupendous class.
5. wizened Comma (2 adjectives) Do not capitalize spelling No comma (little old)	B - a **wizened** little old lady suddenly arrived at the door during spelling C - A **wizened,** little old lady suddenly arrived at the door during spelling.

Vocabulary Word and Skills	Daily Caught'ya (B-for board, C-for correct)
6. portal Apostrophe (contraction)	B - she didnt arrive in the normal way and knock on the **portal** C - She didn't arrive in the normal way and knock on the **portal.**
7. azure Commas (extra information)	B - she just appeared out of the **azure** sky at the classroom side of the door C - She just appeared, out of the **azure** sky, at the classroom side of the door.
8. swirling Commas (2 adjectives, series) No comma for color adj.	B - she wore a long **swirling** black dress a pointed yellow hat and purple shoes C - She wore a long, **swirling** black dress, a pointed yellow hat, and purple shoes.
9. sported Do not start sentence with a conjunction. No comma for color adj.	B - and high over her gray head she **sported** a large purple umbrella with yellow polka dots C - High over her gray head she **sported** a large purple umbrella with yellow polka dots.
10. interrupt Apostrophe (contraction) No capital on spelling.	B - she didnt **interrupt** the spelling lesson C - She didn't **interrupt** the spelling lesson.

Vocabulary Word and Skills	Daily Caught'ya (B-for board, C-for correct)
11. patiently Comma (participial phrase) Abbreviation (Ms., Mr.) Homophone (there)	B - waiting for _____ to finish talking she just stood there **patiently** C - Waiting for _____ to finish talking, she just stood there **patiently**.
12. stared Paragraph Abbreviation (Mr., Ms.) Homophone (their) Comma (appositive, interruptive)	B - all the students however just **stared** at the old lady and ignored _____ there teacher C - All the students, however, just **stared** at the old lady and ignored _____ , their teacher.
13. baffled Keep verb tense the same. Comma (appositive) Abbreviation (Ms., Mr.) Capitalize English	B - _____ the english teacher is **baffled** C - _____, the English teacher, was **baffled.**
14. apparition Question	B - who was this **apparition** C - Who was this **apparition?**
15. blurted Paragraph Capitalize proper nouns	B - _____ and _____ **blurted** out loud C - _____ and _____ **blurted** out loud.

Vocabulary Word and Skills	Daily Caught'ya (B-for board, C-for correct)
16. weird Punctuation (quote) 2 sentences Question and statement	B - who are you you look **weird** they said C - "Who are you? You look **weird,**" they said.
17. responded Paragraph	B - the old lady politely **responded** C - The old lady politely **responded.**
18. piping Punctuation (quote) Homophone (here) Capital (I, begin quote)	B - she said with a **piping** voice i am hear because you are such a good class C - She said with a **piping** voice, "I am here because you are such a good class."
19. diminutive Punctuation (quote) Homophone (here) Capital (I, begin quote)	B - the **diminutive** lady added i am hear to reward you because you are so very good C - The **diminutive** lady added, "I am here to reward you because you are so very good."
20. statement Comma (introductory prepositional phrase)	B - with that **statement** she carefully folded her purple umbrella C - With that **statement,** she carefully folded her purple umbrella.

Vocabulary Word and Skills	Daily Caught'ya (B-for board, C-for correct)
21. unison Paragraph Punctuation (quote) Capital (begin quote)	B - the class cried out in **unison** what are you going to give us C - The class cried out in **unison,** "What are you going to give us?"
22. remonstrated Paragraph Abbreviation (Ms., Mr.) Punctuation (quote) Apostrophe (contraction)	B - thats not polite **remonstrated** _____ C - "That's not polite," **remonstrated** _____ .
23. solicitous Paragraph Capitalize proper nouns Plural (ladies) Comma (appositive)	B - _____ and _____ very **solicitous** young ladys offered the old woman a chair and welcomed her C - _____ and_____ , very **solicitous** young ladies, offered the old woman a chair and welcomed her.
24. focused Strong verb Vocabulary practice	B - all attention **focused** upon the wizened lady C - All attention **focused** upon the wizened lady.
25. crone Paragraph Plural of classes Can avoid quotes with that	B - the old **crone** explained that she was the guardian angel of good classes C - The old **crone** explained that she was the guardian angel of good classes.

Vocabulary Word and Skills	Daily Caught'ya (B-for board, C-for correct)
26. gaunt Commas (series) Write out numbers Strong verbs	B - she snapped her **gaunt** fingers mumbled a few words and blinked 3 times C - She snapped her **gaunt** fingers, mumbled a few words, and blinked three times.
27. materialized Commas (series)	B - a large box **materialized** from out of nowhere floated in the air near her hands and then settled gently to the floor at her feet C - A large box **materialized** from out of nowhere, floated in the air near her hands, and then settled gently to the floor at her feet.
28. pried Paragraph Capitalize proper nouns	B - _____ and _____ **pried** open the box C - _____ and _____ **pried** open the box.
29. miniature, versions Apostrophe (possession)	B - the carton was filled with **miniature versions** of the old ladys umbrella C - The carton was filled with **miniature versions** of the old lady's umbrella.

Vocabulary Word and Skills	Daily Caught'ya (B-for board, C-for correct)
30. enraptured Comma (compound sentence)	B - the girls were **enraptured** by the purple polka-dotted umbrellas and the boys were disappointed C - The girls were **enraptured** by the purple polka-dotted umbrellas, and the boys were disappointed.
31. sufficient Homophone (there) Comma (compound sentence) Vocabulary review	B - there were **sufficient** umbrellas for each pupil in the class but there was none for the teacher C - There were **sufficient** umbrellas for each pupil in the class, but there was none for the teacher.
32. dismayed Paragraph Comma (interjection) Homophone (they're) Capitalize proper nouns	B - eew they're purple umbrellas with yellow dots cried **dismayed** _____ and _____ C - "Eew, they're purple umbrellas with yellow dots!" cried **dismayed** _____ and _____ .
33. interjected Paragraph Punctuation (quote) Capitalize proper noun Homophone (they're) Comma (appositive)	B - there for girls **interjected** _____, another boy in the class C - "They're for girls," **interjected** _____ , another boy in the class.

Vocabulary Word and Skills	Daily Caught'ya (B-for board, C-for correct)
34. taciturn Paragraph Vocabulary review	B - the girls remained *taciturn* and waited for the old crone to finish her story C - The girls remained *taciturn* and waited for the old crone to finish her story.
35. archaic 2 sentences Verb tense agreement	B - the *archaic* lady tells the class that these were not ordinary umbrellas they are magic C - The *archaic* lady told the class that these were not ordinary umbrellas. They were magic.
36. issued Run on	B - each pupil was to be *issued* an umbrella and these umbrellas could take the student wherever he or she wished to go C - Each pupil was to be *issued* an umbrella. These umbrellas could take the student wherever he or she wished to go.
37. chorused Paragraph Punctuation (quote) Comma (series, appositive) Write out numbers Capitalize proper nouns	B - wow *chorused* _____ _____ and _____ 3 boys in the class C - "Wow!" *chorused* _____ , _____ , and _____ , three boys in the class.

Vocabulary Word and Skills	Daily Caught'ya (B-for board, C-for correct)
38. ludicrous Paragraph Homophone (they're) Capitalize proper nouns Punctuation (quote)	B - maybe there not so *ludicrous* after all said ——— C - "Maybe they're not so *ludicrous* after all," said ——————— .
39. astute Paragraph Capitalize proper nouns Write out numbers Comma (appositive) Homophone (their)	B - ———— and ———— 2 *astute* girls in the class noticed that there was no umbrella for there teacher C - ——— and ————, two *astute* girls in the class, noticed that there was no umbrella for their teacher.
40. adults Paragraph Plural of child Verb tense agreement Comma (appositive)	B - the umbrellas were for the childs because they had been so good and not for any *adults* even teachers C - The umbrellas were for the children because they had been so good and not for any *adults,* even teachers.
41. location Homophones (their, there) Commas (series, compound sentence)	B - all the students had to do was close their eyes hold up there umbrellas picture the *location* they wished to go and they would be there C - All the students had to do was close their eyes, hold up their umbrellas, picture the *location* they wished to go, and they would be there.

Vocabulary Word and Skills	Daily Caught'ya (B-for board, C-for correct)
42. astounded Paragraph Punctuation (quote) Apostrophe (contraction) Homophone (it's)	B - its magic said **astounded** C - "It's magic," said **astounded** _____ .
43. urged Paragraph Punctuation (quote) Apostrophe (contraction)	B - lets try it right now **urged** _____ C - "Let's try it right now," **urged** _____ .
44. trilled Paragraph Punctuation (quote) Capitalize I Strong verb	B - wait a minute **trilled** the guardian angel i must warn you first C - "Wait a minute," **trilled** the guardian angel. "I must warn you first."
45. mention No one is two words Avoid quote with that Subject/pronoun agreement	B - she went on to explain that noone must **mention** a word about their umbrellas outside the classroom C - She went on to explain that no one must **mention** a word about his/her umbrella (or the umbrellas) outside the classroom.

Vocabulary Word and Skills	Daily Caught'ya (B-for board, C-for correct)
46. trek Comma (compound sentence) Vocabulary practice Subject/pronoun agreement Homophone (no)	B - know pupil could **trek** anywhere without their teacher and the umbrellas of students who misbehaved would not work for a while C - No pupil could **trek** anywhere without his/her teacher, and the umbrellas of students who misbehaved would not work for a while.
47. queried Paragraph Abbreviation (Ms., Mr.) An before nouns beginning with a vowel Commas (appositive)	B - the students **queried** how _____ their teacher could travel without a umbrella C - The students **queried** how _____ , their teacher, could travel without an umbrella.
48. shrewd Paragraph Homophone (you"re) 2 sentences Apostrophe (contraction) Comma (2 adjectives) Punctuation (quote)	B - your a **shrewd** wonderful class said the old woman youll figure it out C - "You're a **shrewd,** wonderful class," said the old woman. "You'll figure it out."
49. tweaked Commas (introductory prepositional phrase, verb series)	B - with that statement, she smiled **tweaked** her nose closed her eyes and was gone C - With that statement she smiled, **tweaked** her nose, closed her eyes, and was gone.

Vocabulary Word and Skills	Daily Caught'ya (B-for board, C-for correct)
50. persist Punctuation (quote)	B - **persist** in being good she said as her body dissolved into thin air C - **"Persist** in being good," she said as her body dissolved into thin air.
51. pondered Paragraph	B - the students **pondered** and thought C - The students **pondered** and thought.
52. essayed Homophone (their)	B - they **essayed** there umbrellas in the classroom C - They **essayed** their umbrellas in the classroom.
53. reappeared Run on Strong verbs	B - students appeared and **reappeared** all over the room and it was a mess C - Students appeared and **reappeared** all over the room. It was a mess!
54. amiable Paragraph Proper noun Commas (series, appositive) An before a noun beginning with a vowel	B - _____ a **amiable** girl took the teacher by the hand closed her eyes and thought of the corner of the room C - _____ , an **amiable** girl, took the teacher by the hand, closed her eyes, and thought of the corner of the room.

Vocabulary Word and Skills	Daily Caught'ya (B-for board, C-for correct)
55. twinge Comma (compound sentence)	B - she felt a tiny **twinge** but nothing happened C - She felt a tiny **twinge,** but nothing happened.
56. genial Comma (appositive) Apostrophe (possessive)	B - then _____ another **genial** student took the teachers hand on her other side C - Then_____ , another **genial** student, took the teacher's hand on her other side.
57. envisioned Write out numbers Commas (series) Homophone (their)	B - together the 2 students closed their eyes held up there umbrellas and **envisioned** the top of the closet C - Together the two students closed their eyes, held up their umbrellas, and **envisioned** the top of the closet.
58. crouched Paragraph Write out numbers Comma (introductory adverb)	B - suddenly all 3 were **crouched** on top of the closet C - Suddenly, all three were **crouched** on top of the closet.

Vocabulary Word and Skills	Daily Caught'ya (B-for board, C-for correct)
59. screeched Comma (appositive) Proper noun	B - _____ the teacher **screeched** in fear because she was afraid of heights C - _____, the teacher, **screeched** in fear because she (he) was afraid of heights.
60. hastily Comma (2 adjectives)	B - the amiable kind students **hastily** wished themselves back on the floor C - The amiable, kind students **hastily** wished themselves back on the floor.
61. raring Paragraph Comma (subordinate clause) Homophone (their)	B - now that they had discovered how to travel somewhere with there teacher the students were **raring** to go C - Now that they had discovered how to travel somewhere with their teacher, the students were **raring** to go.
62. reluctantly Paragraph Comma (compound sentence, interruptive)	B - the teacher however insisted on finishing the spelling lesson so the umbrellas were **reluctantly** put back in the box C - The teacher, however, insisted on finishing the spelling lesson, so the umbrellas were **reluctantly** put back in the box.

Vocabulary Word and Skills	Daily Caught'ya (B-for board, C-for correct)
63. brief Paragraph Comma (introductory prepositional phrase)	B - after the lesson the teacher decided to try the umbrellas on a **brief** trip C - After the lesson, the teacher decided to try the umbrellas on a **brief** trip.

64. entire
 	
Commas (introductory
  adverbial phrase, verb
  series, extra information)
Write out numbers
Apostrophe (plural
  possessive)
Abbreviation (P.E.)
	B - instead of walking to the pe field the **entire** class with the teacher holding 2 students hands put up their umbrellas closed their eyes and envisioned the pe field
	
	C - Instead of walking to the P.E. field, the **entire** class, with the teacher holding two students' hands, put up their umbrellas, closed their eyes, and envisioned the P.E. field.

65. instantaneously Comma (adverb at the beginning of sentence) Abbreviation (P.E.)	B - **instantaneously** they were all on the pe field C - **Instantaneously,** they were all on the P.E. field.
66. awesome Paragraph Commas (series) Punctuation (quote) Proper nouns	B - **awesome** murmured _____ _____ and _____ C - **"Awesome,"** murmured _____ , _____ , and _____ .

Vocabulary Word and Skills	Daily Caught'ya (B-for board, C-for correct)
67. shrilled Paragraph Punctuation (quote)	B - super **shrilled** all the girls C - "Super!" **shrilled** all the girls.
68. bemoaned Paragraph Comma (interjection) Punctuation (quote)	B - oh my what will the principal think **bemoaned** the teacher to herself C - "Oh my, what will the principal think?" **bemoaned** the teacher to herself.
69. cavorted Paragraph Strong verb	B - the class **cavorted** on the field for a while and then used the umbrellas to return to the classroom C - The class **cavorted** on the field for a while and then used the umbrellas to return to the classroom.
70. inform, boon Paragraph Comma (adverb at beginning of sentence)	B - Meanwhile the teacher was thinking how to **inform** the principal of this **boon** C - Meanwhile, the teacher was thinking how to **inform** the principal of this **boon.**

Vocabulary Word and Skills	Daily Caught'ya (B-for board, C-for correct)
71. exotic Comma (2 adjectives) Proper noun	B - the girls dreamed of far away romantic places with **exotic** names like katmandu C - The girls dreamed of far away, romantic places with **exotic** names like Katmandu.
72. schemed Homophone (their) Vocabulary practice Strong verb	B - the boys **schemed** to get even with there enemies in other classes by materializing on top of them C - The boys **schemed** to get even with their enemies in other classes by materializing on top of them.
73. perturbed, garish, unmanly Vocabulary Comma (2 adjectives)	B - they were still a bit **perturbed** by the **garish unmanly** colors of the umbrellas C - They were still a bit **perturbed** by the **garish, unmanly** colors of the umbrellas.
74. stowed Paragraph Vocabulary practice Comma (introductory prepositional phrases) Homophone (their)	B - at the end of the class all the students reluctantly **stowed** their umbrellas in the box C - At the end of the class, all the students reluctantly **stowed** their umbrellas in the box.

Vocabulary Word and Skills	Daily Caught'ya (B-for board, C-for correct)
75. venture Paragraph Abbreviation (P.E.)	B - the next day the class decided to **venture** farther than the pe field C - The next day the class decided to **venture** farther than the P.E. field.
76. ingenious Commas (appositive, city) Proper nouns Abbreviation (D.C.)	B - _____ the **ingenious** teacher put on the board a picture of the steps of the capital in washington dc C - _____, the **ingenious** teacher, put on the board a picture of the steps of the Capitol in Washington, D. C.
77. image Subject/pronoun agreement	B - everyone put that **image** in their head C - Everyone put that **image** in his/her head.
78. toting Paragraph Proper noun Comma (city, introductory adverb) Hyphen	B - suddenly the entire class of purple umbrella- **toting** students was in washington dc C - Suddenly, the entire class of purple umbrella-**toting** students was in Washington, D.C.

Vocabulary Word and Skills	Daily Caught'ya (B-for board, C-for correct)
79. fashion Vocabulary review Comma (introductory prepositional phrase)	B - in this **fashion** the class made brief visits all over the world C - In this **fashion,** the class made brief visits all over the world.
80. secrecy Paragraph Apostrophe (contraction)	B - one day _____ and _____ just couldnt stand the **secrecy** anymore C - One day_____ and _____ just couldn't stand the **secrecy** anymore.
81. furtively Proper noun Homophone (their) Comma (introductory prepositional phrase)	B - after the last class they slipped they're umbrellas under their jackets and **furtively** left the school C - After the last class, they slipped their umbrellas under their jackets and **furtively** left the school.
82. gadget Spelling (friends) Homophone (their)	B - they thought that they would show all there freinds at home this neat **gadget** C - They thought that they would show all their friends at home this neat **gadget.**

Vocabulary Word and Skills	Daily Caught'ya (B-for board, C-for correct)
83. envious Spelling (friends) Homophone (their)	B - they could envision the **envious** looks on the faces of all there friends C - They could envision the **envious** looks on the faces of all their friends.
84. disbelieving Comma (subordinate clause) Homophone (their)	B - when they got home in a circle of **disbelieving** boys they opened their jackets C - When they got home in a circle of **disbelieving** boys, they opened their jackets.
85. consternation Comma (introductory prepositional phrases) Proper nouns	B - to the **consternation** and embarrassment of _____ and _____ the umbrellas were gone C - To the **consternation** and embarrassment of _____ and _____ , the umbrellas were gone.
86. tormented Write out numbers Comma (participial phrase)	B - the other boys teased and **tormented** the 2 boys saying that they had lied about the umbrellas C - The other boys teased and **tormented** the two boys, saying that they had lied about the umbrellas.

Vocabulary Word and Skills	Daily Caught'ya (B-for board, C-for correct)
87. impulsiveness Write out numbers Comma (compound sentence) Homophones (knew, their) Vocabulary practice	B - the 2 boys new that they had broken the rules of the old crone and they wondered what their **impulsiveness** had cost them C - The two boys knew that they had broken the rules of the old crone, and they wondered what their **impulsiveness** had cost them.
88. adhered Paragraph Comma (subordinate clause) Homophone (their)	B - when they got to school the next day they found that there umbrellas were back in the box and that they had **adhered** to the side C - When they got to school the next day, they found that their umbrellas were back in the box and that they had **adhered** to the side.
89. daily, distributed Write out numbers Comma (subordinate clause) Apostrophe (plural possessive)	B - when the class **distributed** the umbrellas to go on the **daily** trip the 2 boys umbrellas stayed stuck to the side of the box C - When the class **distributed** the umbrellas to go on the **daily** trip, the two boys' umbrellas stayed stuck to the side of the box.

Vocabulary Word and Skills	Daily Caught'ya (B-for board, C-for correct)

90. dispatched
 	
Proper noun
Apostrophe (possessive)
Do not capitalize language
    arts
Commas (appositive,
    compound sentence)
	B - _____ the language arts teacher could not leave the boys alone so she **dispatched** them to the principals office
	
	C - _____ , the language arts teacher, could not leave the boys alone, so she **dispatched** them to the principal's office.

91. clemency Paragraph Abbreviation (Ms., Mr.) Commas (appositive, participial phrase)	B - _____ the principal showed **clemency** toward the boys figuring that they had suffered enough C - _____ , the principal, showed **clemency** toward the boys, figuring that they had suffered enough.
92. penitent Write out numbers	B - the 2 boys were so **penitent** that the principal bought them ice cream C - The two boys were so **penitent** that the principal bought them ice cream.
93. discovered Paragraph Homophone (their)	B - the next day the boys **discovered** that there umbrellas no longer adhered to the box C - The next day the boys **discovered** that their umbrellas no longer adhered to the box.

Vocabulary Word and Skills	Daily Caught'ya (B-for board, C-for correct)
94. remainder Paragraph Apostrophe (possessive) Proper noun Comma (introductory prepositional phrase) Strong verb Abbreviation (Ms., Mr.)	B - for the **remainder** of the year _____ s class traveled all over the world with the umbrellas C - For the **remainder** of the year, _____ 's class traveled all over the world with the umbrellas.
95. fascinating Comma (compound sentence)	B - they had many exciting adventures and they met many **fascinating** people C - They had many exciting adventures, and they met many **fascinating** people.

NOTE: *At this point you may wish to go into some amusing detail about some of the adventures. You may want to go to wherever your students are studying in social studies. Make something funny happen there.*

| 96. revisited

Paragraph
Apostrophe (possessive)
Abbreviation (Ms., Mr.)
Strong verb | B - the last day of school the archaic lady **revisited** _____ s classroom

C -   The last day of school the archaic lady **revisited** _____ 's classroom. |

Vocabulary Word and Skills	Daily Caught'ya (B-for board, C-for correct)
97. bussed Commas (series) Strong Verbs	B - she picked up the box of umbrellas **bussed** each student on the forehead and hugged the teacher C - She picked up the box of umbrellas, **bussed** each student on the forehead, and hugged the teacher.
98. profusely Paragraph	B - the polite students thanked the lady **profusely** C - The polite students thanked the lady **profusely**.
99. ancient Paragraph Punctuation (quote) Capital (begin quote) Run on Vocabulary practice	B - the **ancient** crone said you are such a good class and i hope you enjoyed my gift C - The **ancient** crone said, "You are such a good class. I hope you enjoyed my gift."
100. hollered Paragraph Punctuation (quote) Comma (yes, series) Capital (begin quote) Vocabulary practice Strong verbs	B - the entire class **hollered** yes thank you as the old lady closed her eyes put up her purple umbrella with yellow polka dots tweaked her nose and disappeared C - The entire class **hollered**, "Yes, thank you!" as the old lady closed her eyes, put up her purple umbrella with yellow polka dots, tweaked her nose, and disappeared.

100 Sample Caught'yas
"Hairy Beast and Friends"

Grades 6 - 8

CHAPTER 7

Important Notes

In almost every Caught'ya, students will be required to capitalize the first letter of the sentence, supply the end punctuation, and capitalize the proper nouns. These are not, therefore, listed each time in the skills.

Some of the more sophisticated skills, such as subject agreement with pronoun or the use of semicolon are included only once or twice. At the middle school level the purpose is to introduce, not to master these skills. Of course, you can insert more Caught'ya sentences if you want your students to have more practice. While irregular verb forms are used in the sentences, at this level I do not often ask students to correct any irregular verbs in the Caught'yas. The correct form is simply there. I believe that children unconsciously absorb the correct forms of irregular verbs from their language experiences more effectively than from any drill or conscious practice.

There are only one hundred Caught'yas given here. If you do three a week, these one hundred sentences are all that you will need. If you do one Caught'ya a day, you'll need eighty more of them. Having to come up with some of your own gives you the flexibility to add sentences anywhere you wish. You can give more detail to the basic story line for more practice in the skills you determine are necessary.

Sixth grade classes, for example, may need more practice in letter writing format. You can make up a series of Caught'yas with several short letters between Hairy and Hilda. Eighth graders will probably need repetition in the more difficult skills. I usually do this particular story with my seventh graders. They always need more practice in punctuating quotations, and there are lots of places in this story where more conversation can be easily inserted.

In addition, depending on the grade level and the proficiency of your classes, you may wish to simplify or to make more difficult the basic examples provided here. Adapt them to suit your needs. Have fun!

The vocabulary words are intended for fun, extra credit, and enrichment. They are not bound to one grade level. You will notice that some of the same vocabulary words are repeated for the elementary, middle, *and* high school levels. A fourth grader can have just as much fun with a ten-dollar word as a seventh grader or an eleventh grader. The only difference is that older students can use the word in their writing as well as in their speech.

The skills in the one hundred sentences were not taken out of the air. I included the skills from state-adopted grammar books and from the curriculum guide for my county. The skills, however, are threaded through the sentences rather than presented in the usual textbook sequence.

Finally, let me emphasize that the Caught'ya method works. Use these sentences to forge a partnership with your students, a partnership that will result in improved writing, increased vocabulary, and lots of shared laughs.

Vocabulary Word and Skills	Daily Caught'ya (B-for board, C-for correct)
1. regaled Paragraph Capitals (title) Quotes around story	B - every day in this spot you will be **regaled** with news from the dramatic story of general animal hospital. C - Every day in this spot you will be **regaled** with news from the dramatic story of "General Animal Hospital."
2. inoffensive Commas (appositive)	B - hairy beast an **inoffensive** beastie with green fur was a grossly ugly but gentle animal C - Hairy Beast, an **inoffensive** beastie with green fur, was a grossly ugly but gentle animal.
3. comely Comma (appositive)	B - once he was madly in love with hilda hippo a **comely** hippopotamus with a hard heart C - Once he was madly in love with Hilda Hippo, a **comely** hippopotamus with a hard heart.
4. fickle Commas (interrupter) Homophone (too)	B - **fickle** hilda however decided that hairy beast was to ugly for her C - **Fickle** Hilda, however, decided that Hairy Beast was too ugly for her.

Vocabulary Word and Skills	Daily Caught'ya (B-for board, C-for correct)
5. visage Comma (2 adjectives, appositive) Apostrophe (possessive)	B - hilda the mean lady could no longer stand hairys repulsive warty **visage** C - Hilda, the mean lady, could no longer stand Hairy's repulsive, warty **visage.**
6. vituperative Comma (2 adjectives) Starting sentence with a conjunction	B - so she wrote him a nasty **vituperative** letter to tell him of her feelings C - She wrote him a nasty, **vituperative** letter to tell him of her feelings.

7. rue
 	
Letter heading
Commas (city, state, date)
	B - 4321 **rue** street
	        hogtown florida 32609
	        september 5 1989
	
	C - 4321 **Rue** Street
	        Hogtown, Florida 32609
	        September 5, 1989

8. grotesque,
 	
Paragraph
Commas (greeting, closing,
   2 adjectives
Homophones (your, there)
Capitals (greeting,
   closing)
Apostrophe (contraction)
	B - dear hairy
	your a **grotesque** ugly beast. i do not love you. their, thats it!
	hatefully yours
	hilda
	
	C - Dear Hairy,
	      You're a **grotesque,** ugly beast. I do not love you. There, that's it!
	            Hatefully yours,
	            Hilda

Vocabulary Word and Skills	Daily Caught'ya (B-for board, C-for correct)
9. odious Paragraph Comma (date) Spelling (received)	B - hairy beast recieved this **odious** letter on september 8 1990 C - Hairy Beast received this **odious** letter on September 8, 1990.
10. copious Strong verbs Commas (verb series) Simile	B - he cried **copious** tears tore out tufts of green fur and demolished his apartment like a wild beast C - He cried **copious** tears, tore out tufts of green fur, and demolished his apartment like a wild beast.
11. demeanor Commas (verb series) Simile	B - his **demeanor** was like that of a dog who had lost its favorite squeakie toy missed supper and been scolded C - His **demeanor** was like that of a dog who had lost its favorite squeakie toy, missed supper, and been scolded.
12. woebegone 2 Sentences Commas (adjective series verb series) Run on	B - poor sad **woebegone** hairy was totally destroyed and his heart had been broken and stomped on and abused C - Poor, sad, **woebegone** Hairy was totally destroyed. His heart had been broken, stomped on, and abused.

Vocabulary Word and Skills	Daily Caught'ya (B-for board, C-for correct)
13. serpent	B - bertha boa was a sweet thoughtful and kind **serpent**
Paragraph Comma (adjective series)	C - Bertha Boa was a sweet, thoughtful, and kind **serpent**.
14. lament	B - she heard hairys **laments** and she slithered to his apartment to investigate
Strong verbs Comma (compound sentence) Apostrophe (possessive) Go over coordinating conjunctions - and, or, nor, for, so, but, yet	C - She heard Hairy's **laments**, and she slithered to his apartment to investigate.
15. ajar	B - oh boy she found the door **ajar** and a total mess inside but hairy was nowhere to be seen
Commas (interjection, compound sentence) Part of speech (interjection)	C - Oh boy, she found the door **ajar** and a total mess inside, but Hairy was nowhere to be seen.
16. rummaged	B - wow bertha **rummaged** for unfortunate grotesque hairy under the bed in the fridge and behind the boots in the closet
Commas (interjection, series of prepositional phrases, 2 adjectives) Prepositional phrases Strong verb	C - Wow, Bertha **rummaged** for unfortunate, grotesque Hairy under the bed, in the fridge, and behind the boots in the closet.

Vocabulary Word and Skills	Daily Caught'ya (B-for board, C-for correct)
17. dolorous Commas (2 adjectives, compound sentence) Conjunctions Verb tense agreement	B - bertha searched everywhere and could not find hairy yet she still hears ***dolorous*** sobs echoing through the trashed messy apartment C - Bertha searched everywhere and could not find Hairy, yet she still heard ***dolorous*** sobs echoing through the trashed, messy apartment.
18. perturbed Comma (compound sentence) Spelling (friend) Verb tense agreement No comma (restrictive modifier)	B - bertha became really ***perturbed*** so she goes back to her apartment to write a note to her friend wilfred warthog C - Bertha became really ***perturbed***, so she went back to her apartment to write a note to her friend Wilfred Warthog.
19. chafe Letter heading Commas (city, state, date)	B - 1234 ***chafe*** street hogtown florida 32609 september 30 1990 C - 1234 ***Chafe*** Street Hogtown, Florida 32609 September, 30 1990

Vocabulary Word and Skills	Daily Caught'ya (B-for board, C-for correct)
20. desolated Paragraph Capitals (greeting) Spelling (friend) Homophones (our/are) Comma (greeting) Letter format No comma (restrictive modifier)	B - dear wilfred what is wrong with are freind hairy beast. he seems to have been **desolated** by something C - Dear Wilfred, What is wrong with our friend Hairy Beast? He seems to have been **desolated** by something.

21. console
 	
Apostrophes (contractions)
Comma (closing, compound sentence)
Capitals (closing)
Letter format
	B - lets try to **console** him and maybe hell come out of hiding
	               love
	               bertha
	
	C - Let's try to **console** him, and maybe he'll come out of hiding.
	             Love,
	             Bertha

22. epistle Paragraph Conjunctions (go over) Comma (compound sentence, 2 adjectives)	B - wilfred thought that bertha had a good idea so he wrote hairy a short consoling **epistle** C - Wilfred thought that Bertha had a good idea, so he wrote Hairy a short, consoling **epistle**.

Vocabulary Word and Skills	Daily Caught'ya (B-for board, C-for correct)
23. dross Letter heading Commas (city, state, date)	B - 6543 **dross** street hogtown florida 32609 october 2 1990 C - 6543 **Dross** Street Hogtown, Florida 32609 October 2, 1990

24. chum
 	
Paragraph
Capitals (greeting, closing)
Run on
Spelling (friend)
Commas (direct address,
    interjection,
    greeting, closing)
Homophone (your)
	B - dear hairy
	well old **chum** where have
	you been and what is wrong
	with you that you can't
	answer you're door are you
	all right
	        your freind
	        wilfred
	
	C - Dear Hairy,
	    Well, old **chum**,
	where have you been?
	What is wrong with you
	that you can't answer
	your door? Are you all
	right?
	        Your friend,
	        Wilfred

25. pompous Paragraph Comma (compound sentence) No apostrophe in plural	B - wilfred wrote hairy the **pompous** note and bertha sent him a bouquet of flower's C - Wilfred wrote Hairy the **pompous** note, and Bertha sent him a bouquet of flowers.

Vocabulary Word and Skills	Daily Caught'ya (B-for board, C-for correct)
26. agitatedly Paragraph Verb tense agreement Commas (subordinate clause, interruptive)	B - when the doorbell rang hairy hoping it was news from hilda crept out from his hiding place in the bathtub and **agitatedly** answers the door C - When the doorbell rang, Hairy, hoping it was news from Hilda, crept out from his hiding place in the bathtub and **agitatedly** answered the door.
27. inadvertently Conjunctions Comma (compound sentence) Apostrophe (possessive)	B - he adored the flowers from bertha but he was insulted by wilfreds **inadvertently** unkind note C - He adored the flowers from Bertha, but he was insulted by Wilfred's **inadvertently** unkind note.
28. vilified Run on Commas (series) Spelling (friend)	B - hairy felt overwhelmed and he had been jilted by his girl insulted by his freind and had his warts **vilified** C - Hairy felt overwhelmed. He had been jilted by his girl, insulted by his friend, and had his warts **vilified**.

Vocabulary Word and Skills	Daily Caught'ya (B-for board, C-for correct)
29. anew Comma (participial phrase) Simile Compound verb	B - he burst **anew** into tears. then he shredded the flowers and ate them tears flowing onto the stems like rain C - He burst **anew** into tears. Then he shredded the flowers and ate them, tears flowing onto the stems like rain.

30. atone
 	
Paragraph
Practice vocabulary
Comma (adverb at
  beginning of sentence,
  compound sentence)
	B - luckily wilfred realized that his epistle might have been pompous and he went to visit hairy to **atone** for his booboo
	
	C - Luckily, Wilfred realized that his epistle might have been pompous, and he went to visit Hairy to **atone** for his booboo.

31. saturated Apostrophe (possessive) Commas (yes, subordinate clause, participial phrase) Spelling (friend)	B - yes when he arrived at hairys apartment wilfred found his freind on the floor **saturated** in his own tears C - Yes, when he arrived at Hairy's apartment, Wilfred found his friend on the floor, **saturated** in his own tears.

Vocabulary Word and Skills	Daily Caught'ya (B-for board, C-for correct)
32. remnants Apostrophe (possessive) Strong verb	B - the **remnants** of berthas flowers hung from hairys lips C - The **remnants** of Bertha's flowers hung from Hairy's lips.
33. gaffe, woe Verb tense agreement Commas (verb series) Homophone (to) Apostrophe (possessive)	B - wilfred gathered hairy up in his arms apologized for his **gaffe** and listens too hairys tale of **woe** C - Wilfred gathered Hairy up in his arms, apologized for his **gaffe**, and listened to Hairy's tale of **woe**.
34. plummet Paragraph Punctuation (quote) Apostrophe (contraction) Capital (quote)	B - wilfred then said lets go tell that nasty nerd of a hippopotamus to **plummet** off a cliff C - Wilfred then said, "Let's go tell that nasty nerd of a hippopotamus to **plummet** off a cliff."
35. sniveled Paragraph Punctuation (quote) Capital (quote)	B - hairy **sniveled** yes! C - Hairy **sniveled**, "Yes!"

Vocabulary Word and Skills	Daily Caught'ya (B-for board, C-for correct)
36. persevere Paragraph Punctuation (quote) Apostrophe (contraction) Comma (direct address)	B - then lets **persevere** hairy said wilfred C - "Then let's **persevere**, Hairy," said Wilfred.
37. abode Paragraph Comma (compound sentence) Apostrophe (possessive)	B - hairy and wilfred then went to hildas **abode** and they boldly knocked on the door C - Hairy and Wilfred then went to Hilda's **abode**, and they boldly knocked on the door.

38. raucous
 	
Commas (subordinate
    clause, verb series, 2
    adjectives)
Proper noun (Bronx)
Verb tense agreement
	B - when hilda answered the door hairy showed her all his warts stuck out his tongue and sounds a loud **raucous** bronx cheer
	
	C - When Hilda answered the door, Hairy showed her all his warts, stuck out his tongue, and sounded a loud, **raucous** Bronx cheer.

Vocabulary Word and Skills	Daily Caught'ya (B-for board, C-for correct)
39. loathed Paragraph Comma (direct address) Punctuation (quote) Run on Capital (quote) Verb tense agreement	B - hard-hearted hilda still *loathed* hairy and she slams the door and shrieked get out of my life you vile beast C - Hard-hearted Hilda still *loathed* Hairy. She slammed the door and shrieked, "Get out of my life, you vile beast!"
40. umbrage Pronoun (subject) Apostrophe (possessive) Word order Use of semicolon	B - hairy took *umbrage* at hildas cruel words so him and wilfred went to see bertha C - Hairy took *umbrage* at Hilda's cruel words; Wilfred and he went to see Bertha.
41. bewailed Paragraph Punctuation (quote) Comma (yes at beginning of sentence) Apostrophe (contraction)	B - yes lets go right now *bewailed* hairy C - "Yes, let's go right now," *bewailed* Hairy.
42. trekked Paragraph Strong verb Apostrophe (possessive)	B - they *trekked* to berthas abode and rang the bell C - They *trekked* to Bertha's abode and rang the bell.

Vocabulary Word and Skills	Daily Caught'ya (B-for board, C-for correct)
43. salutations Paragraph Punctuation (quote) Comma (direct address)	B - bertha answered the door. **salutations** hairy and wilfred she greeted C - Bertha answered the door. "**Salutations**, Hairy and Wilfred," she greeted.
44. remonstrated Paragraph Spelling (friends) Verb tense agreement Punctuation (quote) Apostrophe (contraction) Comma (direct address)	B - the three freinds sit down and talked. lets forget about hilda hairy **remonstrated** bertha C - The three friends sat down and talked, "Let's forget about Hilda, Hairy," **remonstrated** Bertha.

45. winsome
 	
2 Paragraphs
Commas (interjection,
   direct address)
Apostrophe (contraction)
Capitals (quote, I)
Punctuation (quotes)
	B - wow what a subject to forget said wilfred. bertha said hairy i'll never get over my **winsome** hilda
	
	C - "Wow, what a subject to forget," said Wilfred.
	     "Bertha," said Hairy, "I'll never get over my **winsome** Hilda."

46. lamented
 	
2 Paragraphs
Punctuation (quotes)
Apostrophe (possessive,
   contraction)
Commas (direct address)
Capitals (quotes)
	B - wilfred took hairys hand well help you hairy he said. how wilfred **lamented** hairy
	
	C - Wilfred took Hairy's hand. "We'll help you, Hairy," he said.
	     "How, Wilfred?" **lamented** Hairy.

Vocabulary Word and Skills	Daily Caught'ya (B-for board, C-for correct)

47. clamored
 	
3 Paragraphs
Capitals (quotes)
Punctuation (3 quotes)
Comma (direct address, no)
	B - a trip said bertha. no another girl **clamored** wilfred. stop it my friends cried hairy
	
	C - "A trip," said Bertha.
	      "No, another girl," **clamored** Wilfred.
	      "Stop it, my friends," cried Hairy.

48. seclusion Punctuation (quote) Capitals (I) Comma (2 adjectives)	B - i think ill go into quiet uninterrupted **seclusion** he continued C - "I think I'll go into quiet, uninterrupted **seclusion**, " he continued.

49. abate
 	
Commas (extra information,
   2 adjectives)
Punctuation (quote)
Vocabulary repetition
No paragraph (same person
   speaking)
	B - i want to be left alone all by my lonesome miserable self to **abate** the pain of losing my lovely winsome hilda hairy finished
	
	C - "I want to be left alone, all by my lonesome, miserable self, to **abate** the pain of losing my lovely, winsome Hilda," Hairy finished.

Vocabulary Word and Skills	Daily Caught'ya (B-for board, C-for correct)
50. echoed 2 Paragraphs Punctuation (quotes) Comma (direct address)	B - good idea hairy **echoed** bertha and wilfred together. bye my good friends whispered hairy C - "Good idea, Hairy," **echoed** Bertha and Wilfred together. "Bye, my good friends," whispered Hairy.
51. despondent Paragraph Comma (2 adjectives, subordinate clause)	B - although poor sad hairy was still **despondent** he trekked to the market for food C - Although poor, sad Hairy was still **despondent**, he trekked to the market for food.
52. ambrosial Comma (noun series) Homophone (there) Proper noun of city	B - their he purchased bags of candy cantaloupe and **ambrosial** brussels sprouts C - There he purchased bags of candy, cantaloupe, and **ambrosial** Brussels sprouts.
53. cowered Strong verbs Comma (verb series) Verb tense agreement	B - he then goes home put the food away **cowered** in his closet and shut the door behind him C - He then went home, put the food away, **cowered** in his closet, and shut the door behind him.

Vocabulary Word and Skills	Daily Caught'ya (B-for board, C-for correct)
54. calamitous Paragraph Comma (yes at beginning of sentence, 2 adjectives) Vocabulary repetition	B - yes hairy went into hibernation until he could recover from his **calamitous** unfortunate love affair with the nasty vituperative hilda C - Yes, Hairy went into hibernation until he could recover from his **calamitous**, unfortunate love affair with the nasty, vituperative Hilda.
55. noxious Paragraph Comma (adverb at beginning of sentence, 2 adjectives)	B - meanwhile hilda went her own **noxious** nasty way C - Meanwhile, Hilda went her own **noxious**, nasty way.
56. prime Homophone (their) Comma (appositive)	B - bertha and wilfred continued their lives without they're **prime** friend hairy beast C - Bertha and Wilfred continued their lives without their **prime** friend, Hairy Beast.
57. uttered Paragraph Comma (appositive) Punctuation (quote) Capital (I) Run on	B - hairy the poor thing **uttered** to himself over and over i don't love hilda and i do hate hilda C - Hairy, the poor thing, **uttered** to himself over and over, "I don't love Hilda. I do hate Hilda."

Vocabulary Word and Skills	Daily Caught'ya (B-for board, C-for correct)
58. embroiled Paragraph Homophone (their) Comma (subordinate clause, city, state,) Homophone (their)	B - while all this was going on other inhabitants of hogtown florida were **embroiled** in their own problems C - While all this was going on, other inhabitants of Hogtown, Florida, were **embroiled** in their own problems.
59. ingenuous Compound subject	B - **ingenuous** wilfred and kind bertha discussed the new developments C - **Ingenuous** Wilfred and kind Bertha discussed the new developments.
60. gleaned Paragraph Question mark in quote Comma (direct address city, state) Punctuation (quote)	B - bertha have you **gleaned** any news about the newest inhabitant of hogtown florida asked wilfred C - "Bertha, have you **gleaned** any news about the newest inhabitant of Hogtown, Florida?" asked Wilfred.
61. disclaimed Paragraph Punctuation (quote) Comma (direct address)	B - no wilfred bertha **disclaimed** C - "No, Wilfred," Bertha **disclaimed**.

Vocabulary Word and Skills	Daily Caught'ya (B-for board, C-for correct)

62. retorted
 	
2 Paragraphs
Punctuation (quotes)
Comma (interjection,
   compound sentence)
Apostrophe (contraction)
Spelling (weird)
	B - well his name is eggbert and hes wierd looking *retorted* wilfred. oh asked bertha
	
	C - "Well, his name is Eggbert, and he's weird looking," *retorted* Wilfred.
	    "Oh?" asked Bertha.

63. pendulum
 	
Paragraph
Simile
Comma (interjection,
   compound sentence)
Punctuation (quote)
No comma with 2 adj.
   when one is a color
	B - well he has a long gray nose that hangs down like a *pendulum* and he weighs a ton wilfred continued
	
	C - "Well, he has a long gray nose that hangs down like a *pendulum*, and he weighs a ton," Wilfred continued.

64. homely Paragraph Punctuation (interrupted quote) Comma (2 adjectives)	B - he sounds like a *homely* grotesque elephant cried bertha and i don't want to meet him C - "He sounds like a *homely*, grotesque elephant," cried Bertha, "and I don't want to meet him."
65. ascertained Paragraph Punctuation (quote) Apostrophe (contraction) Comma (direct address)	B - you havent *ascertained* the worst bertha said wilfred C - "You haven't *ascertained* the worst, Bertha," said Wilfred.

Vocabulary Word and Skills	Daily Caught'ya (B-for board, C-for correct)
66. elitist 2 Paragraphs Apostrophe (contractions) Punctuation (quotes)	B - whats that? hes an ***elitist*** C - "What's that?" "He's an ***elitist***."
67. assented 2 Paragraphs Punctuation (quotes) Apostrophe (contractions) Run on Comma (interjection) Exclamation in quote	B - forget about him and we dont need snobs said bertha yeah ***assented*** wilfred. hey lets have a party he added C - "Forget about him. We don't need snobs," said Bertha. "Yeah," ***assented*** Wilfred. "Hey, let's have a party!" he added.
68. dispatched Paragraph Comma (appositive) Run on Homophone (their) Sentence combining Discuss subject/pronoun agreement	B - bertha ***dispatched*** invitations to their party and wilfred dispatched invitations to their party and they even invited hilda the the nasty hippo C - Bertha and Wilfred ***dispatched*** invitations to their party. They even invited Hilda, the nasty hippo.

Vocabulary Word and Skills	Daily Caught'ya (B-for board, C-for correct)
69. expedited Vocabulary practice Comma (appositive 2 adjectives) Spelling (weird)	B - kind sweet bertha even **expedited** an invitation to eggbert the wierd elitist elephant C - Kind, sweet Bertha even **expedited** an invitation to Eggbert, the weird, elitist elephant.
70. fodder Sentence combining Compound subject Run on Homophone (their) Comma (appositive, city, state,)	B - bertha popped popcorn and wilfred popped popcorn to provide plenty of **fodder** for there party the biggest event in hogtown florida all year C - Bertha and Wilfred popped popcorn to provide plenty of **fodder** for their party, the biggest event in Hogtown, Florida, all year.
71. implore Paragraph Comma (subordinate clause)	B - just before the guests began to arrive wilfred phoned hairy beast to **implore** him to come to the party C - Just before the guests began to arrive, Wilfred phoned Hairy Beast to **implore** him to come to the party.

Vocabulary Word and Skills	Daily Caught'ya (B-for board, C-for correct)
72. bemoaned Paragraph Punctuation (quote) Comma (direct address) Apostrophe (contraction)	B - i just dont feel up to it wilfred **bemoaned** hairy C - "I just don't feel up to it, Wilfred," **bemoaned** Hairy.
73. malevolent Run on Apostrophe (contractions) Punctuation (quote) Capitals (title) Underline title of book Homophone (here)	B - im reading a good book hear in my closet and its called the **malevolent** and nasty hippopotamus and it fits my mood C - "I'm reading a good book here in my closet. It's called <u>The</u> **Malevolent** <u>and</u> <u>Nasty</u> <u>Hippopotamus</u>, and it fits my mood."
74. abandon Paragraph Homophone (our) Apostrophe (contraction) Punctuation (quote)	B - **abandon** that stupid book and come to are party. itll do you some good insisted wilfred C - "**Abandon** that stupid book and come to our party. It'll do you some good," insisted Wilfred.
75. vegetate Punctuation (quote) Apostrophe (contractions) Homophone (your) Comma (direct address)	B - wheres you're backbone man you cant just sit and **vegetate** in a closet for the rest of your life he added C - "Where's your backbone, man? You can't just sit and **vegetate** in a closet for the rest of your life," he added.

Vocabulary Word and Skills	Daily Caught'ya (B-for board, C-for correct)
76. pondered Paragraph Punctuation (quote) No comma (subordinate clause at end)	B - you have a point conceded hairy as he **pondered** a lonely existence without hilda C - "You have a point," conceded Hairy as he **pondered** a lonely existence without Hilda.
77. plethora Paragraph Homophone (there) Comma (direct address, 2 adjectives) Punctuation (quote)	B - hairy as an added attraction there will be a **plethora** of lovely female animals said wilfred C - "Hairy, as an added attraction there will be a **plethora** of lovely, female animals," said Wilfred.
78. bustle Paragraph Abbreviation (O.K.) Punctuation (quote) Comma (interjection, direct address) Homophone (there) Spelling (friend)	B - ok ill **bustle** over their you nice freind concluded hairy C - "O.K., I'll **bustle** over there, you nice friend," concluded Hairy.

Vocabulary Word and Skills	Daily Caught'ya (B-for board, C-for correct)
79. cronies Paragraph Comma (adverb at beginning, city) Subject/pronoun agreement (each, his/her)	B - meanwhile bertha greeted several **cronies** from around hogtown florida. each one had brought their homemade goodies to share C - Meanwhile, Bertha greeted several **cronies** from around Hogtown, Florida. Each one had brought his or her homemade goodies to share.
80. hors d'oeuvres No compound sentence	B - she introduced everyone and then offered them **hors d'oeuvres** and punch C - She introduced everyone and then offered them **hors d'oeuvres** and punch.
81. conversed Strong verbs Proper noun (Panasonic) Clause at end = no comma	B - the guests **conversed** while music blared from the panasonic speakers C - The guests **conversed** while music blared from the Panasonic speakers.
82. score Apostrophe (possession) Quotes (song title) Proper noun (Aerosmith) Comma (compound sentence)	B - someone played aerosmiths angel and a **score** of hip animals began to boogie C - Someone played Aerosmith's "Angel," and a **score** of hip animals began to boogie.

Vocabulary Word and Skills	Daily Caught'ya (B-for board, C-for correct)
83. chandelier Paragraph No compound sentence Comma (introductory prepositional phrase)	B - about an hour later wilfred discovered that someone had plugged the toilet with popcorn and hung strands of spaghetti from the ***chandelier*** C - About an hour later, Wilfred discovered that someone had plugged the toilet with popcorn and hung strands of spaghetti from the ***chandelier***.
84. giddily No compound sentence Capital (begin quote) Run on Paragraph Punctuation (quote)	B - he noticed that several animals laughed ***giddily*** and threw popcorn at each other and this is getting out of hand he moaned C - He noticed that several animals laughed ***giddily*** and threw popcorn at each other. "This is getting out of hand," he moaned.
85. beady Paragraph No comma (subordinate clause at end) Run on	B - at that point he noticed hilda and she was dancing with eggbert as she gazed into his ***beady*** eyes C - At that point he noticed Hilda. She was dancing with Eggbert as she gazed into his ***beady*** eyes.

Vocabulary Word and Skills	Daily Caught'ya (B-for board, C-for correct)
86. simpered Paragraph Comma (direct address, city, state) Homophone (you're) Punctuation (interrupted quote) Run on	B - oh eggbert she **simpered** your the best dancer and dresser in hogtown florida and i've never met anyone like you before C - "Oh, Eggbert," she **simpered**, "you're the best dancer and dresser in Hogtown, Florida. I've never met anyone like you before."
87. conceit, nonchalantly Paragraph Punctuation (quote) Comma (interjection) Spelling (conceit)	B - yeah i know he answered with **conceit** as he **nonchalantly** flexed his muscles C - "Yeah, I know," he answered with **conceit** as he **nonchalantly** flexed his muscles.
88. quashed 2 Paragraphs No comma (bell bottoms) Punctuation (quote) Homophone (you're) Apostrophe (contraction) Hyphen (bell-bottoms)	B - just then hairy arrived in his striped bell bottoms. wilfred **quashed** a chuckle and said your just in time. im going to need help taming this group C - Just then Hairy arrived in his striped bell-bottoms. Wilfred **quashed** a chuckle and said, "You're just in time. I'm going to need help taming this group."

Vocabulary Word and Skills	Daily Caught'ya (B-for board, C-for correct)
89. slovenliness Paragraph Strong verb Comma (introductory prepositional phrase) Run on	B - hairy spied hilda dancing on top of the coffee table with eggbert and at that moment he realized her ***slovenliness*** C - Hairy spied Hilda dancing on top of the coffee table with Eggbert. At that moment, he realized her ***slovenliness***.
90. swooned Paragraph Simile Comma (verb series) Apostrophe (possessive)	B - hilda saw hairy spun around and ***swooned*** in eggberts outstretched arms. she was as light as a tank C - Hilda saw Hairy, spun around, and ***swooned*** in Eggbert's outstretched arms. She was as light as a tank.
91. mocked Paragraph Punctuation (quote) Capital (begin quote) Hyphen (bell-bottoms)	B - eggbert whispered into her ear get a look at the ugly dude in the bell bottoms he ***mocked*** C - Eggbert whispered into her ear. "Get a look at the ugly dude in the bell-bottoms," he ***mocked***.
92. torrid Paragraph No comma (love affair)	B - thus began the ***torrid*** love affair between hilda and eggbert C - Thus began the ***torrid*** love affair between Hilda and Eggbert.

Vocabulary Word and Skills	Daily Caught'ya (B-for board, C-for correct)
93. scoop Paragraph Comma (adverbial phrase, city, state,)	B - Several weeks after the party hogtown florida buzzed with the latest **scoop** C - Several weeks after the party, Hogtown, Florida, buzzed with the latest **scoop**.
94. rapscallions Numbers (write out if two words or less)	B - the 2 **rapscallions** had broken up C - The two **rapscallions** had broken up.
95. jilted 2 Paragraphs Proper noun (Tibet) Punctuation (quotes) Apostrophe (contraction)	B - hilda fell for eggbert and got **jilted** bertha told hairy. shes taking off to go to tibet to see if she can change. oh replied hairy C - "Hilda fell for Eggbert and got **jilted**," Bertha told Hairy. "She's taking off to go to Tibet to see if she can change." "Oh," replied Hairy.
96. interjected Paragraph Apostrophe (plural possessive) Punctuation (quote)	B - all the animals lives will be better off without her **interjected** wilfred C - "All the animals' lives will be better off without her," **interjected** Wilfred.

Vocabulary Word and Skills	Daily Caught'ya (B-for board, C-for correct)
97. staunch Paragraph Punctuation (quote) Comma (direct address) Numbers (write out) Spelling (friend)	B - i love you bertha and wilfred said hairy. you 2 are my **staunch** freinds C - "I love you, Bertha and Wilfred," said Hairy. "You two are my **staunch** friends."
98. shunned Paragraph Word order Comma (interjection, series) Homophone (their) Pronoun (subject)	B - wow hairy finally **shunned** hilda. him and bertha and wilfred happily continued there lives C - Wow, Hairy finally **shunned** Hilda. Bertha, Wilfred, and he happily continued their lives.
99. escapade Paragraph Punctuation (quote) Apostrophe (contraction) Homophone (you're)	B - ill be back for another **escapade** thought hilda as her plane took off. your not rid of me yet C - "I'll be back for another **escapade**," thought Hilda as her plane took off. "You're not rid of me yet."
100. snooty Paragraph Comma (city, state, non-restrictive modifier)	B - all the animals in hogtown florida except mean hilda and **snooty** eggbert wish you a good vacation C - All the animals in Hogtown, Florida, except mean Hilda and **snooty** Eggbert, wish you a good vacation.

100 Sample Caught'yas

"Romeo and Juliet Revisited and Revised"

Grades 9 - 11

Important Notes

In almost every Caught'ya, students will be required to capitalize the first letter of the sentence, supply the end punctuation, and capitalize the proper nouns. These are not, therefore, listed each time in the skills.

Some of the more sophisticated skills, such as dangling modifiers are included only once or twice. The purpose is to introduce, not to master these skills. Of course, you can insert more Caught'ya sentences if you want your students to have more practice. While irregular verb forms are used in the sentences, I do not often ask students to correct them in the Caught'yas. I believe that students unconsciously absorb the correct forms of irregular verbs from their language experiences more effectively than from any drill or conscious practice. You can, of course, write in more verb practice for your students. This would be especially good at the upper levels.

There are only one hundred Caught'yas given here. If you do three a week, these one hundred sentences are all that you will need. If you do one Caught'ya a day, you'll need eighty more of them. Having to come up with some of your own gives you the flexibility to add sentences anywhere you wish. You can give more detail to the basic story line for more practice in the skills you determine are necessary.

Ninth grade classes, for example, may need more practice in punctuating quotations. You can make up a series of Caught'yas with more conversation between Romeo and Juliet. Eleventh graders will probably need repetition in the more sophisticated skills. I use this particular story with my advanced eighth graders. They find these Caught'yas rather challenging.

In addition, depending on the grade level and the proficiency of your classes, you may wish to simplify or to make more difficult the basic examples provided here. Adapt them to suit your needs. Have fun!

The vocabulary words are intended for fun, extra credit, and enrichment. They are not bound to one grade level. You will notice that some of the same vocabulary words are repeated for the elementary, middle, *and* high school levels. A fourth grader can have just as much fun with a ten-dollar word as a seventh grader or an eleventh grader. The only difference is that older students can use the word in their writing as well as in their speech.

The skills in the one hundred sentences were not taken out of the air. I included the skills from state-adopted grammar books and from the curriculum guide for my county. The skills, however, are threaded through the sentences rather than presented in the usual textbook sequence.

Finally, let me emphasize that the Caught'ya method works. Use these sentences to forge a partnership with your students, a partnership that will result in improved writing, increased vocabulary, and lots of shared laughs.

Vocabulary Word and Skills	Daily Caught'ya (B-for board, C-for correct)
1. regaled Paragraph No comma (tragic tale) Comma (appositive) Hyphen (2 related adjectives) Write out 1 and 2 word numbers	B - every day in this spot you will be **regaled** with a sentence or 2 from the revised tragic tale of romeo and juliet 2 star crossed lovers of long ago C - Every day in this spot you will be **regaled** with a sentence or two from the revised tragic tale of Romeo and Juliet, two star-crossed lovers of long ago.
2. lugubrious Apostrophe (possessive) Comma (parenthetical expression) Run on	B - this story however is a less tragic version of shakespeares **lugubrious** tale and it is set in modern times with several new twists C - This story, however, is a less tragic version of Shakespeare's **lugubrious** tale. It is set in modern times with several new twists.
3. tragedy Comma (city, state)	B - much of the action takes place at the verona mall in a town called **tragedy** florida C - Much of the action takes place at the Verona Mall in a town called **Tragedy**, Florida.

Vocabulary Word and Skills	Daily Caught'ya (B-for board, C-for correct)
4. meager Paragraph Spelling (friend) Comma (2 adjectives not age or color, adverbial phrase)	B - one fine sunny day a lovely young lady named juliet capulet took her **meager** clothing allowance and went to the verona mall with a freind C - One fine, sunny day, a lovely young lady named Juliet Capulet took her **meager** clothing allowance and went to the Verona Mall with a friend.
5. encountered Strong verbs Homophone (their) Comma (subordinate clause)	B - when the two girls arrived at the mall they **encountered** some other classmates from there school C - When the two girls arrived at the mall, they **encountered** some other classmates from their school.
6. exultant Paragraph Punctuation (quote) Comma (noun series, direct address) Apostrophe (contraction)	B - helena ophelia miranda cordelia and cressida lets all go shopping cried **exultant** juliet C - "Helena, Ophelia, Miranda, Cordelia, Cressida, let's all go shopping!" cried **exultant** Juliet.

Vocabulary Word and Skills	Daily Caught'ya (B-for board, C-for correct)
7. plethora 2 Paragraphs Punctuation (quotes) Comma (yes at beginning of sentence) Apostrophe (contractions)	B - yes lets said cressida i have a **plethora** of money to spend on clothes this month. ill bet you do groaned helena C - "Yes, let's," said Cressida. "I have a **plethora** of money to spend on clothes this month." "I'll bet you do," groaned Helena.
8. misers Paragraph Punctuation (quote) Comma (direct address) Apostrophe (possessive)	B - my parents are such **misers** miranda whispered juliet i wish i had cressidas money C - "My parents are such **misers**, Miranda," whispered Juliet. "I wish I had Cressida's money."
9. dispersed Paragraph Dangling modifier Comma (long participial phrase) Split verb	B - after purchasing a red skirt a striped blouse and a pair of pink shorts juliet's monthly clothing allowance had all been **dispersed** C - After purchasing a red shirt, a striped blouse, and a pair of pink shorts, Juliet had **dispersed** all her monthly allowance.

Vocabulary Word and Skills	Daily Caught'ya (B-for board, C-for correct)
10. noisome Paragraph Comma (introductory adverb, appositive) Write out 1 and 2 word numbers	B - suddenly over the loudspeaker a voice announced that the band the **noisome** trio would be playing in the center of the verona mall at 4 o'clock C - Suddenly, over the loudspeaker, a voice announced that the band, The **Noisome** Trio, would be playing in the center of the Verona Mall at four o'clock.
11. exuberant 2 Paragraphs Punctuation (quote) Homophone (hear) Comma (interjection, direct address) And replaces comma	B - wow lets go here them cried **exuberant** and broke juliet come on girls. awesome said cressida C - "Wow, let's go hear them!" cried **exuberant** and broke Juliet. "Come on, girls." "Awesome," said Cressida.

12. trekked, perky
 	
3 Paragraphs
Strong verb
Write out numbers
Punctuation (quotes)
Homophone (there)
	B - the 6 girls **trekked** to the center of the mall. their might even be dancing said **perky** helena. there may be some cute boys added cressida
	
	C - The six girls **trekked** to the center of the mall.
	   "There might even be dancing," said **perky** Helena.
	   "There may be some cute boys," added Cressida.

Vocabulary Word and Skills	Daily Caught'ya (B-for board, C-for correct)
13. blaring 2 Paragraphs Comma (subordinate clause, direct address, compound sentence, interjection) Apostrophe (contraction, possessive)	B - as the girls arrived at the malls center the band was **blaring** and some kids were already jiving. oh lets boogie girls sang juliet C - As the girls arrived at the mall's center, the band was **blaring**, and some kids were already jiving. "Oh, let's boogie, girls," sang Juliet.
14. amphitheater 2 Paragraphs Comma (introductory prepositional phrase) Run on (make 3 sentences) Punctuation (quote) Homophone (whole) Strong verbs	B - suddenly juliet froze and the hole mall seemed to stop moving and from across the **amphitheater** a pair of baby blue eyes bored into hers. oh she breathed C - Suddenly Juliet froze. The whole mall seemed to stop moving. From across the **amphitheater**, a pair of baby blue eyes bored into hers. "Oh!" she breathed.

Vocabulary Word and Skills	Daily Caught'ya (B-for board, C-for correct)
15. dapper, besotted 2 Paragraphs Apostrophe (contraction) Comma (appositive, direct address) Spelling (friend) Punctuation (quote)	B - romeo a **dapper** young man with many freinds had frozen as well. he was **besotted** by the beauty of the girl. i'm in love mercutio he murmured to his pal C - Romeo, a **dapper** young man with many friends, had frozen as well. He was **besotted** by the beauty of the girl. "I'm in love, Mercutio," he murmured to his friend.
16. visages 2 Paragraphs Comma (compound sentence, interjection) Write out numbers Homophone (their) Punctuation (quote)	B - everything between the 2 young people seemed to vanish and they approached each other with love stamped on there **visages**. oh hes a doll wailed cressida C - Everything between the two young people seemed to vanish, and they approached each other with love stamped on their **visages**. "Oh, he's a doll," wailed Cressida.

Vocabulary Word and Skills	Daily Caught'ya (B-for board, C-for correct)

17. oscillated
 	
3 Paragraphs
Strong verbs
Homophone (their)
Punctuation (quotes)
Capitals (proper noun)
	B - romeo and juliet ignored their friends and **oscillated** to the music. where do you go to school asked romeo. shakespeare high school replied juliet
	
	C - Romeo and Juliet ignored their friends and **oscillated** to the music.
	    "Where do you go to school?" asked Romeo.
	    "Shakespeare High School," replied Juliet.

18. abode Paragraph Verb tense agreement Apostrophe (possessive) 2 sentences	B - the next day a note arrives at the door of juliets **abode** it was from romeo C - The next day a note arrived at the door of Juliet's **abode**. It was from Romeo.
19. enrapture Letter heading format	B - 1234 **enrapture** street tragedy florida 32609 october 4 1990 C - 1234 **Enrapture** Street Tragedy, Florida 32609 October, 4 1990

Vocabulary Word and Skills	Daily Caught'ya (B-for board, C-for correct)

20. comely
 	
Paragraph
Comma (greeting, closing)
Capitals (greeting,
   closing)
	B - dearest juliet
	you are so **comely.** when
	can i see you again
	          adoringly yours
	          romeo
	
	C - Dearest Juliet,
	     You are so **comely.**
	When can I see you
	again?
	         Adoringly yours,
	         Romeo

21. beauteous 2 Paragraphs Punctuation (quotes) Comma (appositive) Apostrophe (contraction) Abbreviation (Mrs.) Who's vs. whose	B - whose that note from asked mrs capulet juliets mother. its from that **beauteous** romeo replied juliet dreamily C - "Who's that note from?" asked Mrs. Capulet, Juliet's mother. "It's from that **beauteous** Romeo," replied Juliet dreamily.
22. rapscallion Paragraph Punctuation (quote) Comma (direct address) Spelling (weird) Apostrophe (contraction)	B - juliet you stay away from that **rapscallion** mrs capulet said hes from a wierd family C - "Juliet, you stay away from that **rapscallion**," Mrs. Capulet said. "He's from a weird family."

Vocabulary Word and Skills	Daily Caught'ya (B-for board, C-for correct)
23. tractable Paragraph Comma (2 adjectives, appositive)	B - juliet sent a return note to romeo via her best friend the sweet *tractable* miranda C - Juliet sent a return note to Romeo via her best friend, the sweet, *tractable* Miranda.
24. anguished Letter heading format Comma (date, city, state)	B - 5678 *anguished* street tragedy florida 32608 october 5 1990 C - 5678 *Anguished* Street Tragedy, Florida 32608 October 5, 1990

25. adverse
 	
Capitals (greeting, closing)
Comma (greeting, closing)
Run on
Paragraph
Spacing for letter
Who / whom
Subject / object
	B - dearest romeo
	my parents are *adverse* to our relationship and what can we do and who can we get to help us
	   all my love juliet
	
	C - Dearest Romeo,
	   My parents are *adverse* to our relationship. What can we do? Whom can we get to help us?
	     All my love,
	     Juliet

Vocabulary Word and Skills	Daily Caught'ya (B-for board, C-for correct)
26. materialized Paragraph Apostrophe (possessive) Verb tense agreement Comma (compound sentence) Strong verbs Run on	B - that night romeo **materialized** under juliets window and she creeps down and they talk in the back yard for hours C - That night Romeo **materialized** under Juliet's window. She crept down, and they talked in the back yard for hours.
27. pompous Paragraph Agree subject and verb Comma (compound sentence, interjection)	B - romeos parents didn't approve of juliet because they thought the capulets were **pompous** and juliets parents thought that romeos family were a bunch of weirdos wow what a mess C - Romeo's parents didn't approve of Juliet because they thought the Capulets were **pompous**, and Juliet's parents thought that Romeo's family was a bunch of weirdos. Wow, what a mess!
28. periodically Paragraph Comma (participial phrase, aside) Homophone (there, their)	B - romeo and juliet **periodically** met whenever possible at the verona mall pretending that they were meeting there friends their C - Romeo and Juliet **periodically** met, whenever possible, at the Verona Mall, pretending that they were meeting their friends there.

Vocabulary Word and Skills	Daily Caught'ya (B-for board, C-for correct)
29. amble Paragraph Apostrophe (possessive) Hyphen Comma (appositive) Homophone (through)	B - one day romeo arrived in the malls parking lot with his cousin the quick tempered benvolio. he planned to **amble** threw the mall with juliet C - One day Romeo arrived in the mall's parking lot with his cousin, the quick-tempered Benvolio. He planned to **amble** through the mall with Juliet.
30. ingenuous, ensued Paragraph Comma (introductory prepositional phrase, appositive) Semicolon	B - at the same time juliets **ingenuous** cousin tyblat was arriving at the mall. the 2 cars crashed a fight **ensued** C - At the same time, Juliet's **ingenuous** cousin, Tybalt, was arriving at the mall. The two cars crashed; a fight **ensued**.
31. cretin Paragraph Punctuation (quote) Comma (direct address) Latter / former No comma (subordinate clause at end)	B - tybalt you lowdown **cretin** take that yelled benvolio at tybalt as he slugged the latter in the chest C - "Tybalt, you lowdown **cretin**, take that!" yelled Benvolio at Tybalt as he slugged the latter in the chest.

Vocabulary Word and Skills	Daily Caught'ya (B-for board, C-for correct)
32. homely Paragraph Punctuation (quote) Homophone (your) Comma (direct address) Apostrophe (possessive) Spelling (weird)	B - benvolio your weird and **homely** just like the rest of your stupid family shouted tybalt as he landed a punch on benvolios chin C - "Benvolio, you're weird and **homely** just like the rest of your stupid family!" shouted Tybalt as he landed a punch on Benvolio's chin.
33. waxed Paragraph Strong verb Comma (participial phrase) Run on Apostrophe (possessive)	B - the fight **waxed** more and more ferocious and romeo insulted by juliets cousin stepped into the battle C - The fight **waxed** more and more ferocious. Romeo, insulted by Juliet's cousin, stepped into the battle.
34. pugnacious Apostrophe (possessive) Comma (compound sentence, appositive) Run on	B - things got out of hand and other **pugnacious** young men joined the brawl and mercutio romeos best friend was one of them C - Things got out of hand, and other **pugnacious** young men joined the brawl. Mercutio, Romeo's best friend, was one of them.

Vocabulary Word and Skills	Daily Caught'ya (B-for board, C-for correct)
35. fray Comma (compound sentence, subordinate clause, direct address) Punctuation (quote) Paragraph (quote)	B - as the **fray** continued people started getting hurt and everyone had forgotten what had started the fight. oh juliet moaned romeo C - As the **fray** continued, people started getting hurt, and everyone had forgotten what had started the fight. "Oh, Juliet," moaned Romeo.
36. prevailed 2 Paragraphs Comma (introductory adverbial phrase) Run on (4 sentences)	B - the police finally arrived and tybalt and mercutio were taken to the hospital and despite the violence of the fray no one had **prevailed** and romeo went to find juliet C - The police finally arrived. Tybalt and Mercutio were taken to the hospital. Despite the violence of the fray, no one had **prevailed**. Romeo went to find Juliet.

Vocabulary Word and Skills	Daily Caught'ya (B-for board, C-for correct)
37. paramour, banished, chided Vocabulary Apostrophe (possessive) Comma (subordinate clause, direct address) Punctuation (quote) Paragraph Split verb	B - before romeo could find his **paramour** his parents arrived on the scene. romeo you are grounded for a month for this. you will also be **banished** to your grandmothers house until you get over this foolish girl they **chided** C - Before Romeo could find his **paramour**, his parents arrived on the scene. "Romeo, you are grounded for a month for this. You also will be **banished** to your grandmother's house until you get over this foolish girl," they **chided**.
38. swine Paragraph Apostrophe (possessive, contractions) Commas (appositive) Punctuation (quote) Homophone (their) Split verb	B - juliets parents had also arrived to find their daughter. never see that **swine** romeo again they said. why dont you go out with that nice boy named paris. hes rich they added C - Juliet's parents also had arrived to find their daughter. "Never see that **swine**, Romeo, again," they said. "Why don't you go out with that nice boy named Paris? He's rich," they added.

Vocabulary Word and Skills	Daily Caught'ya (B-for board, C-for correct)
39. dolorous Paragraph Commas (appositive) Verb tense agreement Apostrophe (possessive)	B - that evening juliets parents hear the **_dolorous_** sobs of their daughter as she cried to her best friend miranda C - That evening Juliet's parents heard the **_dolorous_** sobs of their daughter as she cried to her best friend, Miranda.
40. lamented Paragraph Punctuation (quote) Verb (lie / lay) Comma (direct address)	B - oh miranda what am i going to do she **_lamented_** as she laid sobbing on her bed C - "Oh, Miranda, what am I going to do?" she **_lamented_** as she lay sobbing on her bed.
41. inflamed Punctuation (quote) Simile Write out numbers (1-2 word) Apostrophe (possessive, contraction) Debate run on	B - im worried about that cousin of mine who is like an **_inflamed_** rhinoceros when it comes to his car and i'm also devastated by the fact that romeo is grounded and banished to his grandmothers house 50 miles away C - "I'm worried about that cousin of mine who is like an **_inflamed_** rhinoceros when it comes to his car. I'm also devastated by the fact that Romeo is grounded and banished to his grandmother's house fifty miles away."

Vocabulary Word and Skills	Daily Caught'ya (B-for board, C-for correct)
42. copious Pronoun (subject) Word order Punctuation (quote) Comma (repeated adverbs) Capital (begin quote)	B - juliet continued to shed **copious** tears and added me and him will never never see each other again C - Juliet continued to shed **copious** tears and added, "He and I will never, never see each other again!"
43. discern Paragraph Metaphor Comma (compound sentence, direct address) Punctuation (quote) Apostrophe (contractions) Homophone (your)	B - juliet why dont you ask your battleship of an aunt to help you suggested miranda. shell **discern** what to do and shes always on you're side C - "Juliet, why don't you ask your battleship of an aunt to help you?" suggested Miranda. "She'll **discern** what to do, and she's always on your side."
44. fathom Paragraph Homophone (your) Punctuation (quote) Simile and metaphor Comma (direct address)	B - miranda my friend your right sighed juliet. aunt nurse is like a tank she will **fathom** the problem and keep bulldozing on until it is solved C - "Miranda, my friend, you're right," sighed Juliet. "Aunt Nurse is like a tank. She will **fathom** the problem and keep bulldozing on until it is solved."

Vocabulary Word and Skills	Daily Caught'ya (B-for board, C-for correct)
45. ceased Paragraph Discussion who / whom Hyphen Apostrophe (possessive) Strong verbs Comma (non-restrictive dependent clause) Verb tense agreement	B - juliet **_ceased_** her blubbering and called her aunt who agreed to help the star crossed lovers. aunt nurse plans to go see romeo at his grandmothers house C - Juliet **_ceased_** her blubbering and called her aunt, who agreed to help the star-crossed lovers. Aunt Nurse planned to go see Romeo at his grandmother's house.
46. odious Paragraph Comma (appositive) Write out numbers Apostrophe (possessive) Strong verbs	B - aunt nurse visited romeo and told him what an **_odious_** toad he was to have hurt tybalt juliets cousin. she also arranged a meeting between the 2 lovers at juliets church C - Aunt Nurse visited Romeo and told him what an **_odious_** toad he was to have hurt Tybalt, Juliet's cousin. She also arranged a meeting between the two lovers at Juliet's church.

Vocabulary Word and Skills	Daily Caught'ya (B-for board, C-for correct)
47. prominent Paragraph Comma (2 adjectives, introductory adverb, appositive, city, state) Apostrophe (possessive) Vocabulary review	B - meanwhile juliets snobby pompous parents were trying to get her to go out with paris the rich spoiled son of the most **prominent** people of tragedy florida C - Meanwhile, Juliet's snobby, pompous parents were trying to get her to go out with Paris, the rich, spoiled son of the most **prominent** people of Tragedy, Florida.
48. perturbed, irate Paragraph Metaphor Punctuation (quote) Apostrophe (contraction)	B - id rather die than go out with that arrogant toad cried **perturbed** juliet to her **irate** parents C - "I'd rather die than go out with that arrogant toad!" cried **perturbed** Juliet to her **irate** parents.
49. articulated 2 Paragraphs Comma (interrupter, direct address) Punctuation (quote) Apostrophe (possessive)	B - the next day as arranged by aunt nurse juliet and romeo met at juliets church i want to marry you juliet **articulated** romeo C - The next day, as arranged by Aunt Nurse, Juliet and Romeo met at Juliet's church. "I want to marry you, Juliet," **articulated** Romeo.

Vocabulary Word and Skills	Daily Caught'ya (B-for board, C-for correct)

50. unfledged
 	
2 Paragraphs
Write out numbers
Punctuation (quote)
Homophone (too)
Comma (no, introductory
   prepositional phrase)
Verb tense agreement
	B - they ask the reverend laurence if he would marry them the reverend said no you are to young and **unfledged**. after all juliet is only 14
	
	C - They asked the Reverend Laurence if he would marry them.
	     The Reverend said, "No, you are too young and **unfledged**. After all, Juliet is only fourteen."

51. thwarted Paragraph Homophone (their) Verb tense agreement Comma (participial phrase) Split infinitive	B - **thwarted** in there intentions by there youth romeo and juliet agreed that it is best to just go steady C - **Thwarted** in their intentions by their youth, Romeo and Juliet agreed that it was best just to go steady.
52. buss Homophone (their) Comma (introductory) prepositional phrases) Write out numbers Vocabulary practice	B - after a brief but passionate **buss** on the lips the 2 young people parted for there respective abodes C - After a brief but passionate **buss** on the lips, the two young people parted for their respective abodes.

Vocabulary Word and Skills	Daily Caught'ya (B-for board, C-for correct)
53. repugnant Paragraph Run on	B - juliet returned home only to find that her parents had plans for her evening and they had invited the **repugnant** paris to dinner C - Juliet returned home only to find that her parents had plans for her evening. They had invited the **repugnant** Paris to dinner.
54. endured Simile Vocabulary practice	B - juliet **endured** the odious evening with her parents pushing paris at her at every opportunity. she felt like a piece of meat in a pool of piranhas C - Juliet **endured** the odious evening with her parents pushing Paris at her at every opportunity. She felt like a piece of meat in a pool of piranhas.
55. clambered Paragraph Strong verbs Comma (verb series, appositive, parenthetical expression) Apostrophe (possessive) Split verb	B - late that night however romeo **clambered** up the tree under the window to juliets room rapped on the window and was enthusiastically greeted by his love the fair juliet C - Late that night, however, Romeo **clambered** up the tree under the window to Juliet's room, rapped on the window, and was greeted enthusiastically by his love, the fair Juliet.

Vocabulary Word and Skills	Daily Caught'ya (B-for board, C-for correct)
56. deploring Comma (series) Homophone (their)	B - they innocently spent the entire night talking plotting kissing and ***deploring*** there fate C - They innocently spent the entire night talking, plotting, kissing, and ***deploring*** their fate.
57. furtively Comma (subordinate clause) Apostrophe (possessive) Write out numbers of less than 3 words Run on	B - just before the morning sun gently touched the curtains romeo ***furtively*** crept out of the window and he planned to hitchhike to his grandmothers house 50 miles away C - Just before the morning sun gently touched the curtains, Romeo ***furtively*** crept out of the window. He planned to hitchhike to his grandmother's house fifty miles away.
58. coursed 2 Paragraphs Punctuation (quotes) Apostrophe (contraction) Vocabulary review Homophone (through)	B - i love you he murmured as he climbed down the tree. im forever yours whispered juliet threw the tears that ***coursed*** down her visage C - "I love you," he murmured as he climbed down the tree. "I'm forever yours," whispered Juliet through the tears that ***coursed*** down her visage.

Vocabulary Word and Skills	Daily Caught'ya (B-for board, C-for correct)
59. plucky, espied Paragraph Punctuation (quote) Comma (direct address) Homophone (you're)	B - try to endure juliet your a **plucky** girl encouraged romeo when he **espied** the tears C - "Try to endure, Juliet. You're a **plucky** girl," encouraged Romeo when he **espied** the tears.
60. asserted Punctuation (quote) Vocabulary review Apostrophe (contraction, possessive) Comma (compound sentence)	B - this banishment will be over in a few weeks and well work something out romeo **asserted** as he waved a final farewell from under juliets window C - "This banishment will be over in a few weeks, and we'll work something out," Romeo **asserted** as he waved a final farewell from under Juliet's window.
61. surreptitiously Paragraph Abbreviation Apostrophe (possessive)	B - no sooner had romeo **surreptitiously** left the scene than mrs capulet arrived at juliets door C - No sooner had Romeo **surreptitiously** left the scene than Mrs. Capulet arrived at Juliet's door.

Vocabulary Word and Skills	Daily Caught'ya (B-for board, C-for correct)
62. distraught, genial Paragraph Punctuation (quote) Capital (proper noun) Comma (direct address)	B - juliet you have a date tonight to go to a sting concert with that **genial** paris boy she informed her **distraught** daughter C - "Juliet, you have a date tonight to go to a Sting concert with that **genial** Paris boy," she informed her **distraught** daughter.
63. blurted, huff 2 Paragraphs Capital (begin quote) Punctuation (quotes) Apostrophe (contraction)	B - never **blurted** out the sobbing juliet. her mother left in a **huff**. well see about that she flung out C - "Never!" **blurted** out the sobbing Juliet. Her mother left in a **huff**. "We'll see about that!" she flung out.
64. diminutive Paragraph Apostrophe (contraction) Comma (participial phrase, 2 adjectives) Write out numbers	B - being only 14 years old the **diminutive** hysterical juliet couldnt stand the pain and the pressure C - Being only fourteen years old, the **diminutive**, hysterical Juliet couldn't stand the pain and the pressure.

Vocabulary Word and Skills	Daily Caught'ya (B-for board, C-for correct)
65. despondent Underline titles Verb tense agreement Comma (participial phrase, appositive) Strong verbs Capitalization rule for titles	B - **despondent** and depressed juliet decides to run away. she forgot food but remembered to take her favorite book love and marriage C - **Despondent** and depressed, Juliet decided to run away. She forgot food but remembered to take her favorite book, <u>Love and Marriage</u>.
66. adjudged Apostrophe (possessives) Semicolon Homophone (there)	B - juliet **adjudged** that it would be dangerous to go to her girlfriends houses or to her aunts her parents would find her their C - Juliet **adjudged** that it would be dangerous to go to her girlfriends' houses or to her aunt's; her parents would find her there.
67. chortled 2 Paragraphs Verb tense agreement Punctuation (quote) Apostrophe (possessive) Plurals with ies Homophone (here)	B - that very night she crept out and hides in the families tomb. no one will think of looking for me here she **chortled** C - That very night she crept out and hid in the family's tomb. "No one will think of looking for me here," she **chortled**.

Vocabulary Word and Skills	Daily Caught'ya (B-for board, C-for correct)
68. epistle Paragraph Abbreviation	B - juliet then sent a short *epistle* to romeo via the rev laurence C - Juliet then sent a short *epistle* to Romeo via the Rev. Laurence.
69. mausoleum Letter heading Comma (city, state, date)	B - creepy *mausoleum* capulet church tragedy florida 32612 january 13 1991 C - Creepy *Mausoleum* Capulet Church Tragedy, Florida 32612 January 13, 1991
70. empathize Paragraph Capitals (greeting, closing, I) Comma (greeting, closing) Vocabulary practice Run on Homophone (here) Apostrophe (contractions, possessive) Line up closing with heading	B - my dearest romeo i am hear in my families mausoleum and please come and bring me food and lets run away and my parents dont *empathize* with the way i feel and well survive somehow all my love juliet C - My Dearest Romeo, I am here in my family's mausoleum. Come and bring me food. Let's run away. My parents don't *empathize* with the way I feel. We'll survive somehow. All my love, Juliet

Vocabulary Word and Skills	Daily Caught'ya (B-for board, C-for correct)
71. awry Paragraph Comma (compound sentence) Vocabulary review Homophone (to)	B - juliets epistle went **awry** and no one came too bring her food C - Juliet's epistle went **awry**, and no one came to bring her food.
72. crypt Paragraph Homophone (too) Comma (subordinate clause, adjective phrase) Verb tense agreement	B - while juliet was starving in the family **crypt** to proud to admit defeat everyone is getting very concerned about her whereabouts C - While Juliet was starving in the family **crypt**, too proud to admit defeat, everyone was getting very concerned about her whereabouts.
73. cadavers Paragraph Pronoun (agreement with subject) Apostrophe (possessive)	B - it was the reverend laurence who found juliet in the mausoleum when he went to pray over there ancestors **cadavers.** C - It was the Reverend Laurence who found Juliet in the mausoleum when he went to pray over her ancestors' **cadavers**.

Vocabulary Word and Skills	Daily Caught'ya (B-for board, C-for correct)
74. frantic 2 Paragraphs Apostrophe (contraction) Punctuation (quotes)	B - ill call you're parents immediately he said. they are **frantic** with worry he added no juliet screamed C - "I'll call your parents immediately," he said. "They are **frantic** with worry," he added. "No!" Juliet screamed.
75. famished Paragraph Comma (participial phrase) Split infinitive	B - neglecting to tell him how **famished** she was juliet pleaded with the reverend laurence to not reveal her hiding place C - Neglecting to tell him how **famished** she was, Juliet pleaded with the Reverend Laurence not to reveal her hiding place.
76. beseeched, wrath Paragraph Punctuation (quote) Capital (I) Apostrophe (possessive)	B - please tell romeo where i am she **beseeched.** we can face our parents **wrath** together C - "Please tell Romeo where I am," she **beseeched**. "We can face our parents' **wrath** together."

Vocabulary Word and Skills	Daily Caught'ya (B-for board, C-for correct)
77. supplications Paragraph Apostrophe (possessive) Abbreviation Comma (participial phrase) Verb tense agreement	B - moved by juliets **supplications** the rev laurence sends a proper note to romeo C - Moved by Juliet's **supplications**, the Rev. Laurence sent a proper note to Romeo.

78. divine
 	
Letter heading format
Comma (city, state, date)
	B - capulet church
	    13 **divine** street
	    tragedy florida 32612
	    january 15 1991
	
	C - Capulet Church
	    13 **Divine** Street
	    Tragedy, Florida 32612
	    January 15, 1991

79. lineage
 	
Inside address format
Comma (city, state)
Abbreviation
	B - romeo montague
	    135 **lineage** avenue
	    drama florida 32808
	
	C - Romeo Montague
	    135 **Lineage** Ave.
	    Drama, Florida 32808

Vocabulary Word and Skills	Daily Caught'ya (B-for board, C-for correct)

80. languishing
 	
Letter format
Paragraph
Capitals (greeting closing)
Punctuation (greeting)
Apostrophe (possessive)
Spelling (truly)
	B - dear romeo juliet is **languishing** away in her parents crypt waiting for you. please come quickly yours truely reverend laurence
	
	C - Dear Romeo,
	      Juliet is **languishing** away in her parents' crypt waiting for you. Please come quickly.
	          Yours truly,
	          Reverend Laurence

81. dearth Paragraph Apostrophe (possessive) Vocabulary practice Spelling (truly) Comma (subordinate clause)	B - while juliets family was going nuts juliet was truely languishing in the tomb from the **dearth** of food C - While Juliet's family was going nuts, Juliet was truly languishing in the tomb from the **dearth** of food.

82. giddy
 	
Comma (compound sentence
  2 adjectives)
Spelling (finally)
Go over coordinating
  conjunctions - and, or,
  nor, for, so, but, yet
	B - she felt **giddy** and lightheaded and she finaly dropped off into a deep dreamless sleep
	
	C - She felt **giddy** and lightheaded, and she finally dropped off into a deep, dreamless sleep.

Vocabulary Word and Skills	Daily Caught'ya (B-for board, C-for correct)
83. hoofed Paragraph Strong verb Write out numbers Comma (participial phrase)	B - romeo not finding any transportation except his own 2 feet **hoofed** it 50 miles to the church C - Romeo, not finding any transportation except his own two feet, **hoofed** it fifty miles to the church.
84. berating Vocabulary review Comma (participial phrase) Homophones (through, whole) Pronoun agreement (subject)	B - he trekked all threw the night and most of the next day **berating** himself the hole time for their stupidity in fighting C - He trekked all through the night and most of the next day, **berating** himself the whole time for his stupidity in fighting.
85. rebuked Paragraph Punctuation (quote) Apostrophe (contractions) Capital (I) Comma (subordinate clause) Wouldn't have been (syntax error)	B - why did we all fight over such a stupid thing as a car accident he **rebuked** himself. if i hadnt fought i wouldnt of been banished he thought C - "Why did we all fight over such a stupid thing as a car accident?" he **rebuked** himself. "If I hadn't fought, I wouldn't have been banished," he thought.

Vocabulary Word and Skills	Daily Caught'ya (B-for board, C-for correct)
86. ajar Paragraph Simile Run on Verb (lie /lay) Comma (subordinate clause) Verb tense agreement	B - when romeo arrived at the crypt he finds the door **ajar.** he peeked in and saw juliet laying motionless like a corpse on a blanket on top of one of the tombs C - When Romeo arrived at the crypt, he found the door **ajar.** He peeked in and saw Juliet lying motionless like a corpse on a blanket on top of one of the tombs.
87. macabre Paragraph Punctuation (quote) Homophone (to)	B - yuck he shuddered what a **macabre** place too hide C - "Yuck!" he shuddered, "What a **macabre** place to hide."

88. harebrained
 	
Punctuation (quote)
Comma (2 adjectives,
   direct address)
No comma (subordinate
   clause at end)
	B - my poor **harebrained** juliet what have you done he continued as he gently kissed her forehead
	
	C - "My poor, **harebrained** Juliet, what have you done?" he continued as he gently kissed her forehead.

Vocabulary Word and Skills	Daily Caught'ya (B-for board, C-for correct)
89. alluring Paragraph Comma (participial phrase) Vocabulary review Verb lie / lay	B - exhausted after his long trek on foot romeo lay down on the blanket next to his **alluring** paramour and went to sleep C - Exhausted after his long trek on foot, Romeo lay down on the blanket next to his **alluring** paramour and went to sleep.
90. slumber Paragraph Comma (verb series, introductory prepositional phrase) Vocabulary practice Run on	B - after a few hours of peaceful **slumber** juliet awoke with her stomach growling and she espied romeo next to her kissed his nose and searched his pockets for the candy bar that she knew he always carried C - After a few hours of peaceful **slumber**, Juliet awoke with her stomach growling. She espied Romeo next to her, kissed his nose, and searched his pockets for the candy bar that she knew he always carried.
91. fortified Comma (participial phrase) Verb (lie /lay)	B - **fortified** with the candy juliet laid down next to romeo and went back to sleep C - **Fortified** with the candy, Juliet lay down next to Romeo and went back to sleep.

Vocabulary Word and Skills	Daily Caught'ya (B-for board, C-for correct)
92. adolescents, callow Paragraph Write out numbers Comma (adverb at beginning) Homophones (their, too)	B - meanwhile the reverend laurence realized that the 2 **adolescents** were to **callow** to be able to solve there horrendous problem themselves C - Meanwhile, the Reverend Laurence realized that the two **adolescents** were too **callow** to be able to solve their horrendous problem themselves.
93. striplings Comma (compound sentence) Strong verbs Homophone (their)	B - he called the montagues and the capulets and he told them to go to the crypt at the church to find there **striplings** C - He called the Montagues and the Capulets, and he told them to go to the crypt at the church to find their **striplings**.

Vocabulary Word and Skills	Daily Caught'ya (B-for board, C-for correct)
94. shrilly 2 Paragraphs Comma (verb series) Verb (lie/lay) Punctuation (quote) Homophone (their) Verb tense agreement Abbreviation	B - both sets of parents arrived at the same time looked inside the mausoleum and gasped in horror at the sight of their children laying on the tomb. there dead mrs montague **shrilly** shrieks C - Both sets of parents arrived at the same time, looked inside the mausoleum, and gasped in horror at the sight of their children lying on the tomb. "They're dead!" Mrs. Montague **shrilly** shrieked.
95. ludicrous Paragraph Punctuation (interrupted quote) Vocabulary review Comma (no at beginning, compound sentence) Continued quote	B - no there not said reverend laurence calmly as he came up behind the distraught parents but they may be if this **ludicrous** situation continues C - "No, they're not," said Reverend Laurence calmly as he came up behind the distraught parents, "but they may be if this **ludicrous** situation continues.

Vocabulary Word and Skills	Daily Caught'ya (B-for board, C-for correct)
96. obdurate 2 Paragraphs Write out numbers Punctuation (quotes) Comma (yes) Apostrophe (contractions) Homophone (they're, too) Abbreviations	B - its time we acted like the adults we are said mr montague yes there both nice youngsters said doctor capulet we were being to **obdurate** C - "It's time we acted like the adults we are," said Mr. Montague. "Yes, they're both nice youngsters," said Dr. Capulet. "We were being too **obdurate**."

97. beau
 	
Paragraph
Vocabulary review
Comma (verb series, direct
    address, introductory
    prepositional phrase)
Apostrophe (possessive)
	B - at that point juliets growling stomach woke her up again. she glanced at both sets of parents shook romeo and said wake up my sweet **beau** and our parents are here
	
	C - At that point, Juliet's growling stomach woke her up again. She glanced at both sets of parents, shook Romeo, and said, "Wake up, my sweet **beau**. Our parents are here."

Vocabulary Word and Skills	Daily Caught'ya (B-for board, C-for correct)
98. enveloped 2 Paragraphs Verb tense agreement Punctuation (quote) Abbreviation Apostrophe (plural possessive) Split verb	B - the surprised youths are immediately **enveloped** in their worried parents arms you may date each other if it means this much to you sighed mrs capulet C - The surprised youths immediately were **enveloped** in their worried parents' arms. "You may date each other if it means this much to you," sighed Mrs. Capulet.
99. trooped Paragraph Punctuation (quote) Apostrophe (contraction, possessive)	B - alls well that ends well said the reverend laurence as they all **trooped** off to have a big dinner at the montagues house C - "All's well that ends well," said the Reverend Laurence as they all **trooped** off to have a big dinner at the Montagues' house.
100. nonsensical Paragraph Comma (adjective series, appositive) Apostrophe (possessive) Quotations marks (title) Homophone (tale) Apostrophe (possessive)	B - thus ends the revised modernized and **nonsensical** tail of shakespeares play romeo and juliet C - Thus ends the revised, modernized, and **nonsensical** tale of Shakespeare's play, "Romeo and Juliet."

CHAPTER 9

Caught'ya Again

While I do not claim that the Caught'ya will, like the proverbial snake oil, cure all the ills of every English class, it certainly does solve a plethora of problems. (Please note correct use of the vocabulary word, and give me extra credit.) That first few minutes of any class period, especially at the elementary or middle school level, usually is spent settling the students down to work. The Caught'ya eliminates that wasted time. Students very quickly get used to beginning work on the Caught'ya even before the bell rings because they want that feedback. The quicker they complete the sentence, the quicker their teacher can get to their side. I have found that because there is less time for horseplay, discipline problems often are averted.

Speaking of discipline, the age-old bugbear of schoolteachers, I have found that the Caught'ya system of grammar really does reduce discipline problems! Why? The closer you are to your students emotionally, the fewer discipline problems you tend to have. My students and I share something. We share a giggle, a daily poke in the shoulder, a back and forth teasing, a plot that few others know about. It's like having a friend in common.

The shared Caught'ya story works on students in somewhat the same way a delightful, elderly neighbor of mine solved a problem with one of my three sons. My youngest son, urged on by his peers, loved to torment the old lady's dog. The dog was a chow and prone to yap and bark ferociously at the slightest provocation. My son poked sticks through the fence and made the chow bark. He threw things at the dog to make it mad. He teased the poor animal until it was frantic.

The elderly lady, distressed at the discomfort of her dog and afraid that my son would harm her precious pooch, walked over to our house one day to talk about the problem. She suggested that she invite my son to her house for tea.

My son, forced by his angry mother, went grudgingly to our neighbor's house. At the door she welcomed him like a grandson. She served my son not only tea and homemade cookies, but a big plate of affection and friendship. She introduced him to the dog. They petted it, fed it, and played with it. When my son returned home, he felt as if he had made two friends. He never teased the dog again. In fact, he stopped other neighborhood boys from playing pranks on the neighbor and her dog.

My son could not torment the lady or her dog any more because they had ceased to be impersonal; they had shared something special. When they had been just symbols, "neighbor and dog," it was easy to tease and play pranks. When the neighbor became a person and the dog had a name, it was out of the question to annoy or to hurt them. Most children have an innate sense of fairness toward persons with whom they have rapport.

The Caught'ya works the same way. Obviously, you still have to maintain some distance from your students, but the Caught'ya provides a shared bond.

One of the highlights of my nearly two-decade teaching career occurred a few years ago. A young man who was known as a terror in most of his classes never misbehaved in mine. Why was I so lucky? Why didn't he wreak havoc in my classroom?

After discussing this student's behavior with several of his other teachers, I became curious. I asked the young man why he didn't interrupt *my* class with his antics. He replied very seriously, "It wouldn't be right. It wouldn't be fair to do that in your class."

It wouldn't have been right because I had become more than a teacher who, like the light in the classroom, is extinguished when you turn off the switch after school, another anonymous fixture in the room. We shared a daily laugh, a story only a few other seventh graders shared, a daily touch — the tea and cookies of the old lady. Other students since that time, in different words, of course, have told me the same thing. I don't promise you that all your discipline problems will disappear, but you will see a relationship develop with your students that all will enjoy.

Pleased by the success of the Caught'ya in my fifth, seventh, and eighth grade English classes, I carried the Caught'ya concept one step further into my French classes. As all foreign language teachers know, one of the difficulties of learning a foreign language is translating from English to the new language. It can be very intimidating, especially if you are only thirteen or fourteen years old.

To solve this problem and to find a quick way to settle my loquacious eighth graders, I use a daily Phrase Féroce (Ferocious Sentence).

The Phrase Féroce is a daily sentence like the Caught'ya, written in English to be translated into French. My students and I complete it in much the same way my English classes complete the Caught'ya. The only problem is that my students (who are only in French I) don't have enough of a French vocabulary to read the complicated sentences necessary to tell a story.

In my French classes, therefore, I abandon the story, but still make the sentences as humorous as I can. I write the sentences every day, basing them on the grammar and vocabulary I had taught the day before. Sometimes a concept is especially difficult for my students (like adjective and noun agreement or direct object pronouns). I repeat this concept daily for months until they are comfortable with it.

This has proved to be an extremely effective method to reinforce and reteach the grammar and the vocabulary that we learn from the textbook. Foreign language textbooks introduce vocabulary and related grammar, provide brief practice exercises, and then move on to the next vocabulary and grammar concepts whether or not the students need more practice in the previous ones. A foreign language teacher cannot linger over a chapter or her students will not be ready for the next level at the end of the year. The Phrase Féroce, which like the Caught'ya takes only five minutes a day, solves this problem. It painlessly cements the concepts and gives much needed reinforcement while still enabling the teacher to cover the entire year's curriculum.

My daily sentences tend to be a critique of myself. "The French teacher is very cruel today," to "My French teacher is an ugly French teacher," or "Mrs. K. is wearing an ugly dress today," and "I'm lucky today; I am going to eat lunch with my strange French teacher in her brown house."

I'm sure you get the idea. While the students don't have a story line to keep them interested and tantalized, they do want to hear my next comment about myself, or my obnoxious dog, or my clothes, and so on. They love it.

Actually the idea of a daily sentence is an old one. Nineteenth-century teachers had their students write one sentence at a time on their slates. Only the story line, the humor, the vocabulary word, and the dramatics are new. You can take my idea, twist it again, and come up with something that may suit your class better than the Caught'ya method described in this book. You are limited only by your imagination!

Now I need to ask you for your help. My fellow teachers and I can come up with only so many story ideas that work with *our* students. If you have an idea or a story that you would like me to use as a basis for a set of one hundred Caught'ya sentences, please send it to me via Maupin House Publishing, P.O. Box 90148, Gainesville, Florida 32607. All story ideas would be welcome.

One final note. Just enjoy yourself. I hope I have given you an alternative way to teach grammar that is more effective, more laugh-filled than any traditional method. I hope your students enjoy Caught'yas as much as my students do. After you use the Caught'ya method for a few months, I'd like some individual, Caught'ya-style feedback too. If you or your students have any comments or suggestions, positive or negative, please write me via my publisher. After all, we are all in this grammar business together, grimace or giggle.

BIBLIOGRAPHY

1. Atwell, Nancie. *In the Middle - Writing, Reading, and Learning with Adolescents.* Portsmouth: Boynton/Cook Publishers, 1987.

2. Caplan, Rebakah and Deech, Catherine. *Showing Writing - A Training Program to Help Students Be Specific.* Berkeley: University of California Press, 1980.

3. Elgin, Suzette Haden. *The Great Grammar Myth.* National Writing Project Occasional Paper #5. Berkeley: University of California Press, 1982.

4. Haley-James, Shirley and Stewig, John Warren. *Houghton Mifflin English.* Boston: Houghton Mifflin Company, 1988.

5. Kiester, Jane. "Burying Dead Verbs and Reviving Live Ones or All's Fair in Love, War, and the Teaching of Writing in Middle School English." *Visions of Teaching and Learning: 80 Exemplary Middle Level Projects*, Ed. John Arnold. Columbus: National Middle School Association, 1990.

6. Kiester, Jane. *Language and the Newspaper.* Gainesville: The New York Times Publishing Company, 1981.

7. Laird, Charlton, preparer. *Webster's New World Thesaurus.* New York: Simon and Schuster, Inc., 1985.

8. Stein, Jess, ed. in chief. *The Random House Dictionary of the English Language* (Unabridged Edition). New York: Random House, 1967.

9. Vail, Neil and Papenfuss, Joseph. *Daily Oral Language Level 7.* Racine: D. O. L. Publications, 1982.

10. Warriner, John, and Graham, Sheila Laws. *Warriner's English Grammar and Composition.* New York: Harcourt Brace Jovanovich, 1977.

Jane Kiester is the author of the popular Caught'ya! books: *Caught'ya! Grammar with a Giggle; Caught'ya Again! More Grammar with a Giggle; Elementary, My Dear! Caught'ya! Grammar with a Giggle for Grades 1, 2, and 3; Giggles in the Middle: Caught'ya! Grammar with a Giggle for Middle School;* and *The Chortling Bard: Caught'ya! Grammar with a Giggle for High School*, all published by Maupin House. Teachers all

over the country also use her *Blowing Away the State Writing Assessment Test* to help improve their students' scores on state writing assessment tests.

In addition to writing books, Jane has given hundreds of workshops to fellow teachers around the country for the past ten years. Her subject? The same as in her classroom where she happily has taught elementary and middle school for over 30 years — teaching students to write well.

During her many years as a classroom teacher, Jane has served as Grade-level Chairperson and as the chairperson of various departments. She is also a past President of the Alachua County Teachers of English. Jane has been recognized four times by *Who's Who Among America's Teachers*. In 2002 she won Teacher of the Year for her school and Middle School Teacher of the Year for her county.

The Chortling Bard: Caught'ya! Grammar with a Giggle for High School

Jane Bell Kiester

Do your high schoolers become a pack of **mammering joltheads** when you try to teach them grammar and mechanics? Do they get all **onion-eyed** when you tell them to pull out their handbooks and primers? **Bestill** their **beslubbering mewls** — the popular Caught'ya! technique for teaching grammar and mechanics has taken a Shakespearean twist especially for high school! Kiester transforms three of the Bard's plays into adaptable Caught'ya! sentences for high school students at any level. Includes a mix and match menu of Elizabethan swear words, enough Caught'ya! sentences for three school years, a straight-spoken grammar handbook, and exams (with keys) for midterms and the end of the year. 240 pp. 0-929895-25-8. #MH41. **$19.95**.

Razzle Dazzle Writing: Achieving Excellence through 50 Target Skills

Melissa Forney

Eliminate mediocre writing! More than 130 mini-lessons, ready to be reproduced, handed to students, and used with the Target Skill instruction to help elementary students master basic skills. By the author of *The Writing Menu*. 174 pp. 0-929895-48-7. #MH75. **$17.95**.

Teaching Written Response to Text: Constructing Quality Answers to Open-ended Comprehension Questions

Nancy N. Boyles

Content-area assessments are a major part of today's educational landscape. Are your middle-grade students ready to write specific, detailed answers to the state's open-ended questions? Twenty-nine sample questions at three thinking levels build analytical skills and boost student confidence. Nancy Boyles uses many elements of Best Practice to support and extend the reading process for *all* students. 212 pp. 0-929895-50-9. #MH84. **$19.95**.

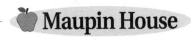 Maupin House

Contact Maupin House for quality on-site professional training.
Free catalog. Phone: 1-800-524-0634 or 352-373-5588
E-mail: info@maupinhouse.com or visit www.maupinhouse.com.
Checks, VISA/MC, or purchase orders accepted.